The Day of the Heart

The Day of the Heart

Michael J. Osborne

Plain View Press
P. O. 42255
Austin, TX 78704

plainviewpress.net
sbright1@austin.rr.com
1-512 441 2452

Copyright Michael J. Osborne, 2005.
All rights reserved.
ISBN: 1-891386-47-6
Library of Congress Number: 2005908029

Art by Charlie Loving.

Other works by Michael J Osborne

Spectra (Spectra Media)

Lease the Wind (Spectra Media)

Silver Haired Daddy (JF&M Media)

Lightland, Climate Change and Human Potential
(Plainview Press, 2000)

Silver in the Mine (Austin Energy Publishing, 2002)

Earthfamilyalpha (Blogspot.com, 2004)

Contents

The Telling	7
Lily	9
The People of the Sun	17
The Day of the Heart	21
The Darkness on the Water	25
Ren	29
The Legend of the White Man	35
The Council of the Elderguides	39
Rom	43
The Gifts of the Arrow	49
Jalar the Terrible	53
The Journey to Argonon	57
The Ways of the Wind People	65
Blackness at Daynight	71
Og	75
The Return	79
The Betrayal	83
Rom the Elk	87
The Wisdom of Evil	91
Madera	95
Preparations	99
The Attack	103
The Door of Destruction	107
The Key	111
The Return to the Tombs	115
The Whirlwind	121
The Liberation	125
Sun Man Moon	129
The End of the Telling	132
About the Author and Artist	135

The Day of the Heart

THE TELLING

Grandmother, Grandmother, tell us a story.
What would you like to hear?
We want you to tell a story we have never heard. A long story.
I know a story, but I cannot tell it in one night.
How many nights will it take?
We will begin tonight just as the moon has reached its fullness.
And when we will finish?
We will finish when the moon once again finds the fullness.

Lily

The soft edge of the sun sits slowly on the golden rims of the great, white Maples along the west shore of the mirrored Lake of Time. Today is like so many other days for Lily. Awake. Arise. Enjoy the air, the breezes, the learning time, the awareness time, and the best of all, the free time when Lily wanders often far from her home and friends in the Pact.

Favorite of her special places is the small pool that gathers water from the spring in the upper meadow below the oak circle. This place is her place of awareness. She selected it three season cycles ago when she became a child person. She remembers the day that her 8th tooth finally fell and her life in the Pact began.

In the far corner of her place, she sees her tree of knowing that she selected as her spirit tree. It has grown, more than she, yet it seems the same. She hears the trickle of the life water as it falls through the cracks in the rocks that fell in the Old Time. She smells the fine hint of the yellow flowers on the crawling vine. She looks to the Sun and feels the world turn. The earth touches her feet.

But today is different somehow. She feels a spirit she has not known. Perhaps it is a smell. Has someone also chosen my place she wonders? But free time ends when the sun touches the earth and her return to Theta 3, although short, is now at hand.

Back in Theta 3, the night ones have finished the day harvest from the garden domes. When Lilly has seen 12 season cycles she too can become a night one. Then, each moon she can light brand the foods to be gathered by the autoharvesters.

ꕤꕥ The Day of the Heart

Lily

But tonight her pact time will be even more special. Tonight, Lily will be a suppermaker. She will watch and learn the ways of the early night from her favorite fatherguide, Rom. Rom is like a great elk on the hill. He is an elderguide and heard by many elderguides in pacthour. It was Rom who taught her that trees are the stitches that hold the earth and the sky together.

At Pactsupper, the suppermakers make the plates of nourishment for each one of the Pact. Although she may offer it any way she chooses, the fun is making it to the most delight of the one she will offer it to. Lily most likes making the plate of nourishment for the Elderguide of Grace. Her skills of delight and mindplay cannot be matched. When Lily brings the Elderguide her favorite green dome beans with a hint of garlic and a slight sprinkle of walnut fruit, her compliments bring Lily new knowledge of word play and thanksgiving. It is an old game that is always new.

"Did you speak to these beans before you brought them to my place of eating," the Elderguide says.

"Of course," says Lily.

"And what did they say?"

"They asked who they were to be given to."

"And you told them?"

"Yes."

"And were they happy about that?"

"Some of them were."

"And the others?"

"They were not so sure."

"Point out which ones to me"

Lily looks a little puzzled. She was playing, but now she is being asked to point out certain beans that in fact never said that they were happy or otherwise.

"Well?"

"I did not really speak to the beans, Elderguide"

"And what about the corn?" says the Elderguide.

"They have ears, do they not."

Lily smiles and serves the plate to the Elderguide, well aware that she has once again found herself in the mindplay of the Elderguide.

ೂ The Day of the Heart

After all the plates of nourishment have been offered, the suppermakers find their places with their fellow homeones.

"This is the night of the day," says the Elderguide of Words. "Without earth, there is no day, without earth there is no night. Without light there is no life. This plate of nourishment is light for our tomorrow, may you take it and use it well. We are thankful for this earth, this light, and this nourishment of earthlight."

It is the job of the elderguide of words to speak at pactsupper, but any elderguide may speak at any time. Childpersons may speak between themselves and the elderguides, but they must keep their voice close to their body.

"Motherone, why does the elderguide speak the same words so often?" asks Lilly.

"His mind is full," says Raiza.

"But if his mind is full why can't he just empty it and make room for more thoughts?"

"The mind is like a great jar that sits out in the world, when it rains it fills. Once it is full, new rain simply falls without mind," says Raiza.

"But what if you break the jar?"

"Then all the wise thoughts will be lost."

"Cannot it be tilted?"

Raiza ponders for a moment, "Yes, but only with care, and remember this jar is very great and not easily tilted without accident or remorse. It is best that elderguides make their jars stable. You must make sure that only the best rain is allowed in your jar. Someday you will find your jar full too."

The songs and talk go on long after Lily must prepare for nightsleep. Her bed is far from the House of Nourishment. The voices and the instruments of the elderguides make a distant hum of life that brings her to quiet sleep in little time. Her homebrothers of more season cycles will play with their e-gear deep into the daynight.

The sun awakes Lily as the birds outside her window finish their morning song. Early day is time for her day work. She rises, cleans her teeth with the sonic brush, brushes her hair, and showers in the sun water. She makes her bed and heads

Lily

for her communicator. From here, she can control the feeding of the animals she cares for. She initiates the water routines for the garden sections she has adopted. She reviews the moisture content around their roots and looks for sign of unfriendly ones who would rather eat the leaves themselves. Lily has chosen to grow only green vegetables this season. She reads her mail from her friends and sees that her good friend Mark in the other valley, the valley of long days, has sent her a good morning video mail.

"Good Morning Lily, I'm finishing my earth science, did you get the last question about the cliff that hangs on the earth?" Lily remembers that she too was confused by the question, and then sends in her earth science mindwork to her mindguide.

Today's mindtime will consist of learning more language, both of her own tongue and of the tongues of many people. She learns of the meaning of the words, how they came to be, and how they have changed over many years. She learns to sign the words with her hands so that she may speak with all who know the universal sign language. Today, Lily will also learn of the physical world and its laws but this takes a mind circle where she can learn with the other Childpersons.

Today's mind circle will be held in the grove of Live Oaks next to the Field of Memories. It is a long walk but a short scoot on her electrobike. She arrives just in time before the circle convenes where she takes her place among her mindcircle friends. She sees Mark and he smiles a boyish hello back. He moves his mouth in that way she knows. It shows something that she knows about Mark, yet she doesn't quite understand how she knows it.

The mindguide stands in the middle of the circle. Her name is Mira and she comes from another Pact that is well known for its knowledge of the world both large and small and for the ability to communicate that knowledge to childones.

"What is the earth?" she says. "Is it dirt? What is this dirt? You say it is mineral or that it is of a life cycle. But we know it is what?"

"Energy," they all chime.

"But why has this energy chosen to be a rock, or a tree, or this dirt. Why has it become what it is?"

༄༅ The Day of the Heart

They search each other for the answer.
What holds this energy together?
"We will hold this question in mind time for another day," says Mira.

Mira then transfers the rest of the day mindwork into the communicators of the mind circle and they each begin work to complete her requests. After the earth has moved the sun from early day to late early day, the circle is broken for this time. Lily and her friends go to their favorites places to share midday nourishment and prepare for their early late day.

Early late day is for the muses. These are the pleasures that transport the person spirit from the cares of this world. There is music and the learning of the instruments. There are the paints and the learning of the brush against the stretched wall of fabric. There is the hammer and the chisel against the living stone. Here the Childpersons learn about their side that is intuitive, the side that is not like the line of the arrow but the meandering of the stream and the endless patterns in the sky. Here, they take their side which is hidden and give it to the creation. They create for creations sake. They dance in the light of the eternal moment.

As late day begins, Lily finds herself with Mark, and her best Childperson friend Morgan. They have gone to the spirit tree that Mark chose when he became a child person.

"Why do they treat us like children," Mark says.

"Because we are children," Morgan responds.

"We will be elderguides soon enough I think," says Lily.

I want to be Childperson as long as I can. I think this is good.

I have heard from Rom that there are those who are not like us who send their children to prisons where their minds are trained to be blind and their hearts are sealed from the sun."

"There is no place of such wrong," says Mark.

"Perhaps so, I wonder?"

The living earth turns the sun to the white bark trees in the west and Lily, Morgan, and Mark return to their Pacts where the serving of the evening plates of nourishment will soon begin.

Thus another day of the People of the Sun is placed into the record of the ages.

🌀 The Day of the Heart

THE PEOPLE OF THE SUN

The People of the Sun came to the Land of Enrichment many years ago. It is said that they were led from the Tombs in the Days of Darkness by a great light that directed their way to the land they now share.

The People of the Sun are simple yet they are not. Their understanding of the world is full. They live in small communities on the land in balance with the forces of nature around them. The Pact is the essential element of their social and spiritual lives. Most Pacts have 100 to 200 elderguides and Childpersons. Theta 3, the Pact where Lily communes, is on the east banks of the Lake of Time, in the Valley of Memories. There are many Pacts in this valley. There is Alpha 9 towards the rising sun, and Beta 7 towards the point star of the turning. There are many other Pacts in the valley and many valleys.

They practice the Way of Living that was given to them by the Ray which brought them from the Tombs. This Way was simple yet profound, uncomplicated, and wise. Each pact is self sufficient. Nourishment comes from gardendomes where livingwater and earthfood is delivered by automated system routines with the helpful watchfulness of the elderguides of nourishment. They manage all the gifts of earth.

Water comes from the skyways which channel the gifts of the sky into the water caverns. The Lake of Time gives its gifts of life through pescaways. These provide the lifemeat for the plates of nourishment. And there are the gifts of the air and the gifts of the land — all for nourishment and for shelter.

The Way of Living provides all things for the Pact. The energy to power their communicators and helpmates comes only from the Sun. Crystals are made by the elderguides of worklight that transform the warmth of the sun into a doingforce. The technology is very old and was found even in the Days of Darkness. The use of crystals for communication, calculation, and workforce is the way of the People of the Sun.

The Sun People live in houses that are soft and flowing. Their life graces the earth. Their life abodes are warm during lowsun

◎ The Day of the Heart

and cool during the season of highsun. Their surfaces change like the light lizard. They invite the warmth of the sun or they ask it away. When it is very cold, the people of the Sun wear their lowsun suits of skin. They are very light yet very warm. When the sun is high, they wear their suits of cooling. These living fabrics of color and touch are more like the living skin of their bearers. They can be cleaned with little effort – even while being on their bearer – a favorite of the childones and for that matter the Motherones too.

There is no dis-ease in the Pact. Sickness, as it is told, was left in the Tombs during the Time of Darkness. Each elderguide will pass from this earth in the time given by the Elderguides' own vision. The Elderguide will only reveal his passing in the moon cycle of its coming.

If a womb elderguide is chosen by the council of elderguides to be a Motherone, the elderguide will quest her spiritvision to guide her in the knowledge of motherness. Sometimes it may be many sun cycles or even moon cycles before the answer will reveal itself. When the spirit vision does reveal itself, the Motherone will go to the Council where she was blessed with the seed of life by the elderguides of life. In 9 moon cycles, she leaves to her place of new life, selected by her, where her newlyborn will be brought into the earth life and the People of the Sun.

All elderguides are as fathers. Childones are of the Pact. Childpersons are in the Pact. The Pact is their family. All people of the sun are brothers and sisters and aunts and uncles and cousins.

The People of the Sun are of a warm skin. Though many are

The People of the Sun

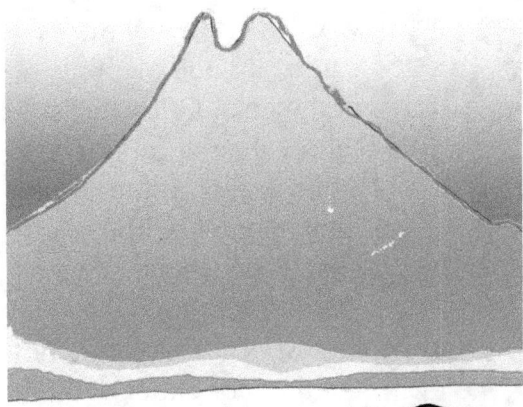

tall, almost all are of strong bone. The hair of the elderguides is long and without waves. The childones grow no hair until they are of the Pact. Elderguides speak with their words only on occasion, using the universal sign language instead. Often they sing or chant during the day. At night, they sing and dance and give thanks together well past the newday hour.

The Way of Life is a meaningful collage of mindwork, musetime, and bodymovement. Even though there is always work to be done, much is given by the cyborgs. These devices and cybersoids provide all of the food, water, and production needed for the Pact. But bodymovement is considered part of the earthlife and many elderguides choose to work in the fields with the cybersoids. Some elderguides roam about the Valley adopting a carerange where they work with the earth to make the natural earthscape its most beautiful. By moving a boulder here, transplanting a tree there, or planting a garden at the foot of a spirit place, the elderguides of the earth slowly and surely turn the whole of the valley into a garden of beauty and balance.

The People of the Sun brought the Sky to the Earth. Unlike the trees that, like stitches, hold the earth and the sky together, the people are like its messengers, the bees, that allow the earth and the sky to talk, to move, and to share their abundance.

Many of the People commune with nature and its life. These Elderguides of Earth talk to the bees, the flowers and the friends of the people who are not human. They understand the cry of the

৩৯ The Day of the Heart

wolf, the moan of the cattle, and the bleating of the goat. Often birds follow them through the valley forest and rest upon their shoulders. They charm the smallest flying life and convince the largest bear that this is not the time for either of them to pass.

The Elderguides of Mater work on their communicators and computators to further the knowledge of the people. They know much of the stars and the heavens and they know much of the smallest things. They build with tiny robots substance from the level of the smallest thing. The fabrics for their life abodes, their tools, their crystals are made from the smallest of the smallest. The elderguides of mater are known for their understanding of all things both great and small.

The Life of the Pact is blessed. The Time of Darkness can be remembered in story only by the Elderguide of Memories. He is the seventh elderguide since the Tombs.

It is the Elderguide of Memories and the Elderguide of Mysteries who know the celebration times. The Elderguide of Mysteries know more than that. Sometimes, it seems, much more.

THE DAY OF THE HEART

The Day of the Heart is the favorite day of Lily and for that matter most of the People of the Sun. It is a special time in the Pact. It comes every moon cycle during the fullness. Lily learned early in her earthscience mind time to know that the Day of the Heart begins at daynight when the moon appears at the turning as the great orb of the sun finds its shadow over the white maples on the Lake of Time.

On the Day of the Heart, the Elderguides serve the evening plates of nourishment to the Childpersons, Motherones, and other members of the Pact. On this evening, the Elderguides of Earth ask that 12 animalfriends give of their time on this earth to become immortal in the life of the Pact.

The Elderguide of Mysteries begins the celebration by facing the dayend. He throws the ashes of those animalfriends, who had given their spirit in the previous mooncycle to the lives of the Pact, into the heavens. With his voice and his hands, he gives thanks to the ghost of oneness from which all is made that can be made. He speaks, "Oh Great Ghost that lives in all that is known, we thank you and honor you. As daynight becomes earthday and darkness becomes light, we give of the heart as we take of your abundance."

Then the Elderguide of Mysteries turns to the side of the turning and speaks to the Moon. He speaks, this time with his hands only, "Ruler of the daynight, open our hearts, and give us strength, to live with courage in life and in death, to grow spirit and love."

Then, he makes a sign that Lily does not know and even her Motherone will not speak of.

ꙮ The Day of the Heart

"What does it mean when The Elderguide moves his hands from his heart and opens them wide then returns to the heart and then up to the sky?"

"It is the Sun Man Moon" says Raiza.

"What does it mean?"

Raiza runs her hand across Lily's forehead. "You must learn that for yourself. No one can teach you. It is the Way of Living."

Lily could not understand how or why the animalfreinds chose themselves or how it came to be that always there were only twelve. This daynight came six clovens and six hooves. Sometimes they were all cloven sometimes all hooves.

The elderguides open the door of immortality and the animals walk in to the place of the giving. Inside, the animals gather into a small herd and then, as if ready for sleep, they all come to rest on the soft hay floor that is covered with beautiful fabrics and colors.

There is a scent of myrrh. The light from the iridescent walls and ceilings begins to fade to near darkness. Then, with a wave of his hands the Elderguide of Mysteries creates a bright cloud of sleep. A soft gentle fog of light ascends from the chamber through a round hole in the top of the place of giving. It twinkles like the daynight sky. It hovers for a moment then moves through the trees and the plants and the rocks and the water.

The elderguides prepare the plates of nourishment and serve them to the Pact at middaynight. Rom serves Lily and Raiza.

"Eat of this plate of nourishment for in it is the spirit of sacrifice and the essence of giving," says Rom.

As the middaynight begins to fall with the turning, each member of the pact stands in the circle of truth and proclaims their gift.

Rom stands and enters the circle.

"Tonight I give my self to all the Childpersons for the next 3 moon cycles. I will teach you, guide you, and comfort you." Lily is thrilled. Rom is always the most fun and in many ways the wisest of all the Elderguides. The next three moon cycles would be full of learning and excitement.

Lily worries about her gift. She could give to a friend, to her Motherone, to the Pact, to the earth, the sky, or even herself if it is

The Day of the Heart

truly a gift of the heart. When it is time for the childones to enter the circle of truth, she still doesn't know what she will say. The Elderguide of Memories places his hand on her shoulder. And what do you give Lily Childperson? "I will give truth," says Lily. "Truth to my friends, the Pact and the heavens"

"Well spoken Childperson," says the Elderguide of Memories. "This is truly a great gift."

As the turning brings the moon to place of hiding, the bright new day begins. There will be no sleeping, for now it is time to begin the giving. The Childpersons surrounded Rom, asking to play earthball. Rom's giving will be a challenge for his patience but a blessing to the opened heart. And that is the purpose of the Day of the Heart . . . to open the heart and to truly love.

The Day of the Heart

DARKNESS ON THE WATER

As the Day of the Heart comes to the end of its time, Lily has just enough free time to visit her place of awareness near the small pool that gathers water from the spring in the upper meadow below the oak circle. She knows from her earthscience mind time that, as the sun finds its shadow over the great white maples, the moon will reveal itself one moon day later at the turning. She stares at the reflection of the great white maples in the pool as the darkness comes over the water.

Lily knows that the last of this Day should be a time of reflection and understanding of the gift of truth that she gave to the Pact.

She wonders what indeed is truth. Is truth wide or is it deep? What if telling the truth causes hurt or harm? If she shares in a mindcircle with her friends, is the truth found in breaking the mindcircle or in keeping it whole?

It is great fun staying up all daynight, but now she yearns for mindsleep. Her eyes are tired yet they see with more wisdom. Her body longs for rest, yet it feels with more heart. She is alert, yet she is almost asleep. She can feel the turning. She can almost hear it. She can also feel something else. Or perhaps it is a smell.

Perhaps it is the mountain laurel that has bloomed just this mooncycle. This is the first mooncycle of the season of beginnings. She hears the beefriends as they finish their workday gathering more fruit from the laurel flowers to bring to their place of living. She remembers the time that she took some of their living work and used it to sweeten Raiza's plate of nourishment. It took courage to do it. She had learned from the Elderguides of Earth how to speak to them and ask them if she could just have a little of their sweet living work. And it did work. Not one angerhurt.

I wonder how my beefriends are doing, she thinks without voicing, *I've got just enough time to go see.*

The beefriend place of living is in an alwaysgreen tree at the foot of the mountain of great hope. As she climbs up the steep slope to find their place she sees her favorite berry tree with many

ꕥ The Day of the Heart
of its berries missing.

"Please my good birdfriends, do not be so greedy. You act like childones who know no moderation."

The alwaysgreen tree grows out of a crack in the earth that becomes a great crack as it moves up the mountain. She has been

Darkness on the Water

in it before. It goes deep into the mountain.

When she arrives she finds the beefriend place of living lying on the earth cracked and despoiled. Who could have done this? The mountain bear? It is not right to disturb a place of living. She looks for tracks in the rocky soil and sees nothing.

But wait, what kind of track is this. Lily has never seen such a track. One large toe behind a triangle shaped hoof. She follows the tracks up to the crevice in the earth. What kind of creature is this?

I should go back to the Pact, she thinks without voicing.

But she continues.

Now the sun has completely taken its shadow and the moon is still not revealed at the turning. Lily reaches for her moon light, but its glow is very low because she has been taking of its light for the entire daynight. Its glow is becoming like the evergrowing daynight sky.

She enters into the black crack in the mountain feeling her way carefully. She speaks into the blackness. "You know, strange creature, it is wrong to wreck a place of living. If you need nourishment, you can ask my beefriends for their living work and they will give you some. If you wreck their place of living, they cannot feed themselves or their childones or you and they will give you angerhurts Shame on you strange creature! I will tell of you to the Elderguides of Earth."

"Please do not tell of me."

Lily feels fear.

"You toungespeak as the People."

"I am hungry and I am weak from the insect bites."

"Who are you strange creature that you speak in our toungespeak?"

"I have come from a place far away."

"Do you need food and planthealings?"

"Yes, but you cannot tell of me. You must promise or I will hide in another mountain."

"I will bring you food and wellgivings when the turning brings the sun to its glory."

"When is that? Are you coming at 9 or at 12 or at 3?"

"I will come as I have told you. Time cannot be counted."

ꕥ The Day of the Heart

REN

Lily carefully finds her way down the earlyslopes of the Mountain of Hope past the pool that gathers water from the spring in the upper meadow below the oak circle. Though she walks with care, her mind is running like the great river that runs into the Lake of Time. Who is this creature with the strange toe behind the hoof who speaks as the People?

When she arrives home, she is exhausted and goes straight to her place of nightsleep. Everyone, including Motherones and elderguides, are tired the daynight after the Day of the Heart. The moon appears at the turning almost as bright as the daynight before. Raiza comes to her place and gives her daynightgifts of water and sweetwords. "Gooddaynight sweet childone, you have done well this passing." As Lily closes her eyes and moves into nightsleep, she remembers her promises. In the distance, she hears Rom singing and proclaiming that all is well in the Pact and for the People of the Sun

As the sun appears at the turning, Lily is up with the birdfriends. She packs her middaynourishment and makes sure she has enough for the strange creature. She also finds the potion of planthealings and pours just enough into her special living jar.

She quickly sees to her own needs and to the needs of the foodplants she has adopted. Everyone is watered and fed. There is no time to see if Mark has sent an imagemessage. Mindcircle will be in the Circle of Truth today.

This day's mindguide is a surprise. Rom is making his gift to the Pact a strong one. For this day, Rom is the mindguide in Lily's mindcircle. Lily's heart grows a measure from this knowledge.

"What is the nature of our existence," says Rom.

Lily is like a stone of wood.

"What does Rom mean," says Benjamin, Lily's most liked angerone. "Existence is not questioned, it is only lived."

"Perhaps that is the answer," speaks Lily.

"Childones, speak your minds openly so we all might hear," says Rom.

꧁꧂ The Day of the Heart

"I know your words but I know not their meaning Rom," says Benjamin. "So I speak to Lily with small breath, that existence is not questioned, it is only lived."

"And I said that perhaps that's the answer, "added Lily.

"Ahh, good good, and I think much of this answer. I must have mindwork time. Mindcircle is over for now. Go find yourselves and your friends. Go to your place of awareness or a new place of awareness. We will find each other."

Lily is like the hoove in the alwaysgreengrassland.

She rushes out of mindtime and scoots to the pool that gathers water from the spring in the upper meadow below the oak circle.

As she finds herself, she moves deliberately but carefully up the mountain of hope, past the oldberry tree, to the alwaysgreen tree, and up the crevice to the great crack.

"I have brought you your food and your healings," says Lily.

"I have brought you your food and your healings

"I have brought you your..."

"Have you brought anyone else," says the creature.

"I have done as I spoke. Shall I leave them at the opening of the mountain?"

"OK OK, that's fine I suppose."

"You must tell me, creature, what is your name, if you have one?"

"Why must you know my name?"

"Everything has a name."

"I am Rain."

"Ren?"

"Yes, like the water that falls from the sky."

"And from what sector do you come?"

"I come from the dominant sector."

"I only know of alpha-zeta in this valley, but there are many valleys. I commune with Theta 3."

"I come from the Valley of Despair."

"I know of no such valley."

"It is there, let me assure you."

"Why have you come to live in the Mountain of Hope?"

"Because I like the view."

Ren

ಅ The Day of the Heart

"I know your words, but I know not your meaning?"

"I am in this lousy cave, with no food, no health care, no nothing. I haven't had a decent nights sleep in a week and the last time I had a warm bath was the night before that."

Lily knows now that this is no creature, but some lossling that she knows only from stories in her pactcircles. She has fear, but she is calm. She knows something, but she knows nothing.

"I will leave what you need at the opening of the mountain."

"Fine, Fine!"

Lily carefully finds her way down the earlyslopes of the Mountain of Hope to the pool that gathers water from the spring in the upper meadow below the oak circle.

She looks into the water. It is still. The earlyslopes of the Mountain of Hope arise in the mirrored pool. They seem like they are of another world.

A birdfriend drops a berry. The pool is alive with circles. The reflection becomes a memory.

I must speak of this day, says Lily, but only when asked.

That is the truth as I know it.

Lily finishes her day with more mindtime, more freetime, and the evening serving of the plates of nourishment. She is of the Pact, but her heartmind is far away. She is thinking of Ren.

She lies awake in her place of nightsleep. If it were not for mindcircle, I would bring Ren more food and then I could see what kind of lossling she might be. But Rom will be our mindguide and his gift will be great.

Ren 〰

The Day of the Heart

THE LEGEND OF THE WHITE MAN

Lily rises as the sun reveals itself at the turning and runs through her earlydaywork. Mind Circle will be on the grass mound above the trail of memories.

"This day I tell you a tale you have not heard before. But first we must mindtale from the suncycle that has passed. Benjamin has offered that we cannot speak of our existence outside of our lives, that it can only be lived.

"Do we all agree?" says Rom.

The childones are without words. "Allow this learning a little time in your heartminds and we will talk of it when it reveals itself."

This day, I tell you of the legend of the White Man.

"Many sun cycles ago, before the People of the Sun, the world was ruled by the White Man. The White Man was the most dangerous animal on earth. He not only fought and killed the Red Man, the Brown Man, the Yellow Man, and the Black Man, he fought and killed his own as virulently as the others.

"The White Man had much power. He had guns and bombs of all sizes. It is said that a single bomb of White Man could wipe out many valleys and poison many more. He used the power of burning rocks to power his cities. These great cities once covered much of the earth. Every White Man, woman and child had a moving thing of metal to take them to wherever they pleased. These moving things were powered by rock oil that White Man removed from the deepest parts of the earth.

"Many of the White Man had great riches as though they were Kings. But many many more lived on their life work only. Even the poorest had these metal moving things that were as big as this mound itself.

"But like all things that exist, the White Man was not all bad. He invented many things. He invented the first computers, healings for the sick, and he played very hard. The White Man had much music, much sport, and many celebrations. They read

✑ The Day of the Heart

and wrote books and made great stories in light and sound called movies. He even went into the heavens and, it is said, planted a flag on the moon.

They sent their childones to school where they would spend all day in small rooms learning from mindguides."

"I have heard that they would lock the childones up" says Mark.

"I do not know of this, but their mind circle was very different from the mindcircle of the People. Each suncycle, the childones went to the same mindcircle called a school. The school was the building. They had no name for the learning. They only knew teaching. And as they became more dead in their minds, they only knew testing."

"And what were they teached?" says Morgan.

"They learned of many things. Like you, they learned of counting. They learned to read and to write, and of their history, which was their version of the truth. They were taught about small things and big things, and how they could be used."

"But we are white aren't we. Our skin is fair." says Benjamin.

"Are we not White Man People also?"

"The People of the Sun have skin that is fair, but we are not White Man."

"Where did the White Man go?" says Lily.

"That is a great Mystery. It is said that he, despite his great works, was much like a child. The White Man said they worshipped God, but they really worshipped money and fire. Their love of money and power blinded them to the care of the earth. It is said that a great flood brought on by so many fires took away many of the great cities.

"Then they began to war with great weapons. And that poisoned many of their own."

"What is money?" says Morgan.

"It was the way they counted their power. With money they would buy food and shelter and they could buy the time and livingwork of those who did not have much money."

"That sounds like slavery."

"In fact it was, but it was dressed in the cloak of Freedom."

The Legend of the White Man ᓀᐧ

"Why did the slaves not revolt?"

"I suppose many tried, The Elderguide of Memories knows many stories of many brave White Man who tried to free the slaves but like the greatpooltide, slavery returned without fail. Now, I want each of you to go to your place of awareness and finish you mindtime. Send Mira your mindwork. I will find you."

Lily is happy. She scoots to her place and rushes up the Mountain of Hope. Will she able to see Ren? She climbs up past the berry tree and the alwaysgreen tree. She comes to the opening in the earth.

"Ren, I have brought you more nourishment."

Lily stares into the silence.

"Ren, I have brought you more ..."

"What is your name?"

Lily feels surprised. "My name is Lily"

"Have you told of me?"

"No"

"Who would you tell, your mother, your father?

"I would tell Rom"

"And who is Rom?"

"He is an Elderguide. He is the Elderguide of both the Earth and the Sky. Ren, may I enter the darkness so I might see you? I have my moon glow."

"Its a little rough, but come on in. Turn to the right when you get to the split and you will find me."

Lily carefully makes her way with her moonglow illuminating the cool darkwalls of the cave. She finds the place of two directions and takes the way to the right. She takes a few more steps and then she stops. There in the pale light of moonglow sits a woman with clothes she has never seen before, and shoes that make the tracks of a creature. There are great jewels that sparkle on her neck and her fingers. The woman before her, though dirty and worn, is beautiful.

She is a woman of the White Man.

The Day of the Heart

THE COUNCIL OF THE ELDERGUIDES

"Lily, why have you not sent your mindwork to Mira?" speaks Rom.

Rom has come to see Lily in her place of awareness as he said.

"I know you have been in the hole in the earth in the Mountain of Hope. What brings you to wander there during your mindtime?"

"Your Motherone Raiza tells me you have been rising before the sun finds the turning, packing your lunch with much nourishment, and finishing your day work as though your heartmind is the great river that flows into the Lake of Time."

Rom puts his hand on Lily's head and caresses her. "Walk with me."

Lily knows that the words "Walk with me" spoken by an Elderguide means realtalking for a Childperson. Rom and Lily walk around the small pool that gathers water from the spring in the upper meadow below the oak circle.

"I have found a strange creature in the hole in the earth," says Lily. It is like no creature I have known in my earthscience. It has tracks of a toe behind a large hoof. It lives in the hole but it is not well. I have been bringing the creature nourishment and well givings of planthealings for two sun cycles already."

"Have you spoke of this creature with an elderguide?"

"Only now with you Rom"

"Why have you kept this knowledge in your heartmind?"

"Because … Because the creature does not want to be known?"

Rom knows that a repeat word from a Childperson is a sign of wordkeeping. "How does the creature tell you of its wants? Does it speak through your earthmind?"

"No?"

"Does it show fear?"

"Yes?"

"And that is how you know it does not want to be known?"

಄ The Day of the Heart

"No Rom, she tounguespeaks as the People. I think she is a lossling from another valley, but a valley far away."

Rom looks at Lily in a way she has never seen before.

His soft stare into her eyes turns inward. He moves his eyes to the mountains toward the turnstar. He grabs the earth with his both hands and brings it to his face where he smells of it. He is silent. Lily has never known Pactloss before but she fears she is on that path. She speaks without voicing, "Have I broken my vow of truth to the Pact. Will I lose my free time? I should have spoken of this creature on the daycycle I had knowledge of it."

"Does this Lossling have trust in you?" says Rom.

"Yes, she has let me see her in the moonglow."

"You have done well, Lily Childperson," speaks Rom in the voice of wisdom. Go now and finish you mindwork and send it to Mira. I will tell Mira to give you until lateday. When you are finished with your mindwork, give me your story with all of your memories." Do this before Pactsupper."

Lily is relieved of her fear, and happy with Rom's words. Yet she feels some other feeling she has not known. It is not fear, yet her heart works as if she is running her fastest. Her heartmind makes images and thoughts that are not clear. They run across her mindseye as if she is nightsleeping.

Lily scoots to her place of living, excited and happy, confused and unsure. She speaks to no one of the lossling.

At Pactsupper, Rom is of few words. His heartmind is within. As the plates of nourishment become empty, he rises and speaks to the Pact. "We are in need of Council listening. I call for the Council to meet me in the Councilmound as the moon reaches the turning. I request all Great Elderguides to be of this Listening. Earth, Heaven, Mater, Memories, Words, Lifework, Worklight, Mysteries, and Force should all be at the listening."

The Motherones talk close to their body while the Elderguides grow silent.

Lily feels fear again. In her life in the pact, she has never heard a calling of the Great Elderguides. Would Rom tell of her story to all of the Great Elderguides? Why should a lossling be of such stature?

As the moon reveals itself at the turning, Lily is awake in her place of nightsleep.

The Council of the Elderguides ✷

She hears the calling of Rom of the Great Elderguide Council. His voice is low and strong. It hovers in the air like the waterair in the season of Endings.

The councilmound is a round room in the earth. There is a fire in its center and a hole in the top. It is covered in earth and grass and flowers. The door to the councilmound is a hatch in the center of the Pacthall. It is said that there are many doors, but only the great elderguides know of them all. The Council sits in a circle on colorful mats that are as old as the Pact itself. Each mat is special and befitting of the place it holds.

Rom moves to the Center.

He speaks with his hands to the Great Ghost of Oneness. He honors each great elderguide ... Mystery, Earth, The Heavens, Mater, Words, Lifework, Memories, Worklight, and Force.

"I bring a grave matter to the Council," says Rom.

"In the hole in the earth in the Mountain of Hope there is lossling.

I have smelled the earth and listened to the Sky and know that this is no lossling of the People.

It is a lossling of the White Man. A woman"

The Great Elderguides make noises like bears.

"We have seen no White Man for many generations?" says the Elderguide of Memories. "Have you faith in your knowledge?"

"I am sure"

"I perceive this to be a trouble" says the Elderguide of Mysteries.

"In my heartmind, I am certain," says Rom.

"And what is your plan Rom" says the Elderguide of Words.

"I will go to the hole in the earth this daynight, and speak to the lossling." I shall bring Elderguides of Force to watch and take guard care." We should place elderguides with watchful eyes and ears at the four corners of the valley.

"And what of the LightForce?" says the Elderguide of Force.

"We cannot amplify without alarming the Pacts."

"Let me take to the Mountain and return before the moon has rested. Then we will know."

ꕤ The Day of the Heart

ROM

Rom departs from the Councilmound and makes his way to the hole in the earth in the Mountain of Hope. He brings two Elderguides of Force. The Elderguides of Force are chosen because of three gifts. They must be strong, they must have great courage, and they must be of uncommon heart wisdom.

Rom and the elderguides arrive at the small pool that gathers water from the spring in the upper meadow below the oak circle.

They make their way up the earlyslopes of the Mountain of Hope past the berry tree and the alwaysgreen tree that grows from the crack below the hole where the lossling hides.

"Ren! This is Rom, the elderguide of earth and sky.

I must awaken you from your nightsleep.

Ren! This is Rom, the elderguide of earth and sky."

There is not a sound from the blackness.

Ron activates his moonglowstick and moves with great care into the cave.

"Ren! I am coming to greet you. Are you still to the right at the split of the cave?"

A soft voice comes from the darkness, "Are you alone?

"I am only with you in this hole."

Rom finds the split and turns to the right. "Are you awake from your nightsleep?"

"Who could sleep on these rocks with no bed and no bedding?"

Rom takes a few more steps and stops. There before him lies Ren. She has brilliant soft clothes, and bright rings and jewels, and hair that is fair, and shoes with high heels. He has never seen such a woman.

"So, you are Rom?"

"I am Rom the Elderguide of Earth and Sky of the People of the Sun, Pact Theta 3 ... and who are you?"

"My name is Rain."

"And why are you in this cave?"

"I have no other home."

❦ The Day of the Heart

"Where was your home?"

Ren pauses, then rises to face Rom. She looks him in the eye with a softness in spirit yet a hardness in mind. "You know."

"You are a White Man woman." Rom backs away and looks at Ren. "Your clothes, your jewels, your hair, your tounguespeak, and those shoes. I have only heard of your kind from the Elderguide of Memories. How do you walk with that spike on your heel?"

"Carefully."

"Why have you no place of living other than this hole in the earth?"

"I have run away. The cities are now ruled by a man who cares only for himself. The man is consumed with his own power. He is evil."

"The White Man have always been evil."

"I mean evil even for the White Man." Ren walks back away from Rom and turns quickly. "He is going to break the Treaty."

"How do you know?"

"Believe me, I know and that is why I have come."

"To warn us?"

"To give you time."

Rom looks at Ren. His face is like the stone. "You will come to Theta 3. You can stay with the Elderguides of Force. I will speak to the Council so they may hear your words."

Rom and Ren wind their way down the earlyslopes of the Mountain of Hope. They come to the small pool that gathers water from the spring in the upper meadow below the oak circle.

Ren sees the Elderguides of Force. "You said you were alone."

"I said I was in the hole in the earth alone."

"Am I under arrest?"

"I do not know those words, but you will stay with the elderguides until the Council hears of your words and speaks of them."

Rom, Ren and the elderguides make their way to Theta 3.

The moon reflects its last daylight into the daynight.

The daynight will be dark until the sun appears at the turning.

When they find themselves at Theta 3, Rom returns to the

Rom

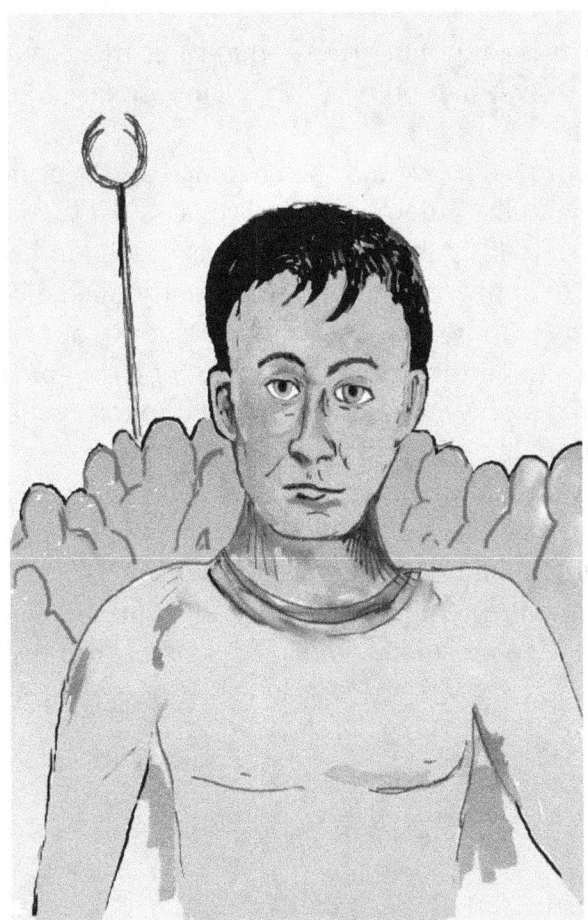

Councilmound. One by one the elderguides come from their place of living and join Rom. Rom is quiet, yet his heartmind is alive with the words of Ren.

"Elderguides, the lossling in the hole in the mountain is indeed a woman of the White Man. She has run way from the Cities. She has brought us a message."

"And what is that message," says the Elderguide of Words.

"The Treaty is to be broken."

The elderguides are without words or signs.

"Why? We have done nothing that would bring about a change from our release. For generations we have lived in our valleys. Why would the White Man break the Treaty?" says the elderguide

ꙮ The Day of the Heart

of mater.

"These words cannot be true. Perhaps it is trick? Why should we believe this woman of the White Man?" speaks the Elderguide of Worklight.

"Bring her to us, so we may see her face and hear her words."

Rom sits with the Elderguides and speaks, "Her words are true, but her heartmind is guarded. The truth is hidden in her. We must listen to our own heartminds and make our judgement.

If the Treaty is to be broken we must tell the Council of Pacts.

The great elderguides go to their place of wisdom. There is a silent buzzing. A light descends from the top of the Councilmound. It rests on the shoulders and foreheads of each great elderguide.

After many breaths, the Elderguide of Mysteries speaks. "So we are all in agreement, the Woman speaks truly. The Pacts must hear of our judgement. The lightforce must be increased. The Woman of the White Man must leave the Valleys of the Sun People."

Rom

The Day of the Heart

THE GIFTS
OF THE ARROW

Rom remains in the Councilmound until the sun reveals itself at the turning. He must go to Ren and tell her of the judgment of great elderguides.

Rom moves like a great elk to the place of living of the Elderguide of Force where Ren has her place of sleeping. He signs the elderguide and enters.

Ren is awake.

"And so Great Rom, what has your Great Council decided?"

"We have judged that your words are true."

"And?"

"There is no and," speaks Rom.

"There is always an and," says Ren.

"You speak wisely. There is no more for you to know."

"Am I to remain locked in this room?"

"No, you are free to be of the Pact for a time."

"And what comes after that?"

"You will return."

"To where?"

"To the Cities."

"You just told me there was no and. This is exactly the kind of and I was talking about. I can't go back to the Cities. Jarlar will cut me up into little filets and feed me to his pets."

"Who is this Jarlar?"

"You people don't pay attention." Ren walks to the window and looks out on the Pact center. There are childones playing on the green earthlawns, Motherones walking and talking, elderguides moving about.

"Your clothes are so, so unstylish."

"They are warm when it is cold and cool when it is warm. What else should they be?"

"Well for one they could have some bright colors." Ren walks over to Rom and runs her finger up the front part of Rom's skin suit. "There is no style here. Here, there could be a very nice

◦◦ The Day of the Heart

collar, and ... perhaps a turn of the fabric here. She steps back and waves her hands in the air. "No big deal just a little nicer to look at. You know what they say clothes make the man."

"We know such saying."

"Well like I guess not. I was told in school that the People of the Sun were weird, and you really are weird."

"So you speak of the People in the Cities."

"Oh yes, we are taught that you people caused a lot of grief, that you made some very powerful people very angry, that you didn't obey the laws, and that you had really funny ideas."

"What ideas?"

"That money is evil. That clocks are bad. That transporters are the destruction of community. You name it. You guys believe some pretty funny stuff."

"It is our way."

"Well it's way out there as far as I can tell."

Ren grabs her colored overgarment and looks in the window and puts on some makeup with the reflection in the glass. "There is not even a mirror in this place. But I guess know one uses them around here right. No reason to look good if there's no reason to look good."

"What do you mean?"

"You know what I mean. Come on, let's get out of this place. I need some sun. That cave wasn't very good for my color."

"But you are white?"

"I paid good money for this tan Pal, here," Ren pulls her pants down below her waist and show Rom her tan. " See this is white, this is tan. Now let's get some sun."

Ren walks do the door, talking to herself, "Sun people who don't get sun, weird."

Rom walks with Ren from the place of living of the elderguide of force. The other elderguides and Motherones pass by them as if Ren was not there. But the childones see.

A childone of 5 full seasons, runs up to Rom and to Ren.

"Who are you?" says the childone.

"She is my friend." speaks Rom.

"Are you an elderguide or a Motherone?" asks the childone.

The Gifts of the Arrow

"She is visiting the Pact from another Valley."

"Why do you look and smell like a flower?"

"Because I like them, says Ren."

The childone looks up at Ren and grins with a smile of the heart, "I like you." Then he runs off as fast as he appeared.

"The children here are full of life," says Ren. "And they seem so happy."

"Their hearts are full and their minds are open."

Rom and Ren walk down the path where the Lake of Time flows into the Gorge of Many Flowers.

"If you like flowers, this way will give you great heartjoy. It will make your eyes run as the river."

"Oh and did I forget to say, you people talk real funny too."

It is the tounguespeak of the People.

"That's what I mean."

"What?"

"What? Oh my God."

Ren and Rom arrive a the Gorge of Many Flowers. It is place where the eldergudes of earth have worked with the plantfriends for many generations. A mist rises from the waterfalls below. It touches each flower and leaf with joy. There are more flowers than in the daynight sky. The fragrance of their joy is everywhere. Ren stares into the Gorge and closes her eyes and takes a large breath. Her face reveals Joy. Tears fall from her eyes.

"This is magnificent! I have never seen anything like it."

"There are many such places of Joy in the Valleys of the People."

Ren turns to Rom and wipes the tears from her eyes.

She looks into his strong eyes. Rom feels her heart with his heartmind. They are silent. Rom feels the turning. His eyes find themselves in the eyes of Ren.

Ren backs away and turns.

"No wonder Jarlar is going to break the Treaty."

"And what is this reason?"

"He needs good gardeners."

ೞ The Day of the Heart

JARLAR THE TERRIBLE

"President Jarlar, we have indications that the Theta 3 Commune in Sector 4 has raised there force field. The rest of the valleys are following suit."

"That would be the first time we've seen that. What does Security think?" President Jarlar gets up from his black steel and glass desk and walks around the desk to his Chief of Staff. He pauses and looks down at the black marble floor. "When was the last time we saw a change in the their force field?"

"According to our records, it's been over a hundred years."

"I wonder what they are afraid of? Jarlar walks to the one of the four windows that allow a magnificent view of the City. "Why did they do it the last time? Anybody know?"

"We believe that there was a rift between the Sun People and the Wind People."

"Have we got anything on satellite?"

"Everything looks normal"

"Tell security to check the council mound with infrared 24 hours before the ramp up and keep a eye on the mound 24/7. What else?"

"You've got your speech before the World Council this afternoon at 3, there is a meeting with the leaders of the Senate late this morning around 11, you've got lunch with the representatives of the robotics union, and tonight you and the Ms. are having a state dinner honoring the recipients of the Golden Star."

"Anything else?"

The Chief of Staff walks over the window where Jarlar is staring at the bustling city filled with transporters and levitons of all shapes, colors, and sizes.

"Your wife was supposed to be back from her nature trip this morning."

"She's always late. Where does her transponder place her?"

"She must have taken it off, it's shows her to be in the same place she was three days ago."

Jarlar turns from the window with a decidedly angry frown

❧ The Day of the Heart

and walks to the front of the presidential desk. " I have told her and told her not to remove her transponder." He slams his fist down on the glass table jarring everything on it, making a loud, reverberating clatter. "She just doesn't get it."

The Chief of Staff grabs his telecomputer and goes to the huge double doors where the President's Royal Guards stand day and night, 24 hours a day.

As he gets halfway down the long distance of Jarlar's cavernous Office of State he stops and turns toward the President. "She's always hated that thing. Security warned you about that before you married her. There were reports that she would take it off even when she was a child. Now that she's your wife, she thinks she can do whatever she wants."

Jarlar looks down at his desk and at the picture of his wife and says, "She's always done what she wants. It's the curse of the beautiful. Anybody else spends 5 years in the Tombs for that. She takes it off as if it was jewelry."

Jarlar walks back to the window and places both hands behind his back. He looks out towards the row of memorials that line the grand avenue leading to his palace. The wind is blowing the flags briskly from the south. It will be very hot today he thinks. The office of environment will probably issue another inside day. If so, it would be the third day in a row and spring has just arrived.

Jarlar's speech to the World Council will be very difficult. Many of the other City Alders are not happy with Jarlar. His "get tough" policy on workers has added many ranks to the Tombs. The Tomb population has grown fivefold since he took control. Just feeding the Tomb population has become a burden for many of the Cities. Plus, he has other problems. The radioactive poisons from the power stations are leaking, but he has kept it a secret. His health minister has given him reports of more and more sickness. He has kept a lid on that too. He is running out of room to hide the sick and dying and he needs to move the power station poisons away from the City.

The Treaty of the Earth requires him to keep his poisons in the City. He thinks to himself, "All those valleys, all that land going to waste. If I just had a good reason to break the Treaty."

Jarlar the Terrible

The Day of the Heart

THE JOURNEY TO ARGONON

Rom and Ren meet in the early day. He wants to show Ren more paths of Joy and the other places of care that the Elderguides of Earth have made with their earthfreinds.

As they walk together, Rom speaks in a low voice, "You must depart from this place."

Ren just keeps walking.

"There is nothing that can be done. The great elderguides will not change their judgement."

Ren stops and looks into Rom's eyes. "You would have me go back to Jarlar? He will put me in the Tombs for the rest of my life for doing what I have done."

"You cannot stay with the People."

"Rom, I cannot go back to the Cities. There is too much sickness, too many people with too little to do except talk of themselves or each other. Even if I was not sent to the Tombs, I do not want to go back. I won't go back!"

Rom gazes off to the mountains rising over the Lake of Time. "There is another way"

"What?"

"The People of the Wind. They are not of the People of the Sun. They have a great earthship many suncycles towards the falling. I have been there once as a child. It is a good place of living. They may give judgement that you can make your place of living with them. Besides, their ways are not so weird, as you say, as the People. They have, what do you call it, style."

Ren thinks for a moment, "And do they speak with the Cities?"

"Yes, but like the People, they do not commune with the White Man."

Rom and Ren walk down the richly flowered garden path to a special clearing.

"Do you see that Great Rock jutting from the earth," asks Rom. That is my place of awareness. When my eighth tooth lost its

☙ The Day of the Heart

place, I went in to the woods to find my place of awareness. After two days, this rock appeared to me. I come here often."

"And what do you do here?"

"I speak to the Ghost of Oneness ... to the earth and to the sky. I go deep into my heartmind. I feel the turning. I find my oneness."

Ren walks to the great rock. "May I?" She rests her back on the smooth jutting rock and leans her back and looks up to the sky.

"This is a very nice place Rom. I like your rock."

Rom walks to Ren and looks down on her as she looks into the sky. "This is not my rock. The People own only their lives, and we give that to the Pact and to the earth so we can grow our hearts"

Ren look back up at Rom, "So what is the name of this earthship?"

"The Wind People speak of it as Argonon."

"Will you take me there?"

Rom knew this question would come. "This I will do. We shall make our way as the turning brings daynight."

As the sun finds its shadow over the Lake of Time, Rom and Ren prepare for their journey. For safety, they will travel with two Elderguides of Force. They will need an earth transporter, something that is rarely seen in the Valley of the Sun.

Ren sees Lily preparing the Plates of Nourishment for the Pact Supper. "Lily, I am leaving now. Thank you for finding me."

"Will you return to the People?"

"I hope so."

Lily signs goodbye and Ren blows a kiss.

Rom signs to the elderguides, the Motherones, and the Childpersons. The elderguide of Mystery signs back.

Good journey. Good journey.

Rom heads for the transporter with Ren and stops and looks back. He looks over at Raiza and signs with her. Then he looks at

The Journey to Argonon

Lily. Lily is courageously holding back the water from her eyes.

"Get your necessaries."

Lily runs to Rom with great surprise and joy. "How did you know?"

"Does not the River flow from the mountains?"

"Rom?" speaks Lily. "It would not be fair if I were the only Childperson to go. More eyes would make stronger memories for those who would want to hear of our journey."

"You speak beyond your years Childperson Lily, and who would be behind these eyes?"

"Whoever you would choose Rom."

"It would not be fair to choose another Childperson of your nature nor would it serve well to have these eyes from the same Pact."

"And so who will it be?"

"I will choose Mark of the Valley of Long Days."

Lily is pleased, but she really wants her best friend Morgan to share the journey.

"And," says Rom, "We shall bring Morgan."

So the Journey begins – Rom, Ren, the elderguides of force, Sheb and Aaron, and the three Childpersons Lily, Mark, and Morgan.

The first daynight of moving is very slow. There are no ways for transporters in the Valleys. Almost all travel in the valleys is by foot or small solar scooters like the one Lily enjoys. The Way of the People has no need of transporters. The valleys are so beautiful, the life is so full, where would one go and why?

Leaving the valleys to go to the Earthship of the Wind People is rare good fortune. This is Lily's first ride in a transporter! Mark is impressed. Rom and Ren ride in the front compartment. Rom makes the course using a wheel. At his feet are two petals. One

ꕥ The Day of the Heart

makes the tranporter go faster, the other makes it go slower. A reflection in the glass displays all kinds of numbers and maps. In the compartment behind what Mark named a cockpit are two seats and a small table. There is room to prepare Plates of Nourishment towards the front and many places for the necessaries of the journey.

Lily, Mark, and Morgan have the compartment to the rear. There are soft fuzzy seats on three sides and a glass wall that moves up and down. It seals the compartment in the rear from the compartment to the front. Mark finds a small switch that controls the glass wall in the in the first moments of the journey.

Out of the Valley of Long Days, to the Valley of Red Trees, to the Valley of Strong Rains, to the Valley of Soft Sun, they make their way.

"Are we almost there," says Morgan.

Rom looks back to the rear of the transporter. "We are two suncycles away. You will know we are close when the valleys are no more and the trees grow like bushes, and the land has much thirst."

During the days, they rest and explore. But they take care to remain under the trees. Lily does not know why but she has the wisdom to keep her wonder to herself.

After two suncycles, the trees grow small and the mountains change.

"Why do these mountains have flat tops," says Mark.

"These are high flatlands that have given themselves to the wind and the water," replies Rom. "If you look with care, you can see the earthship of the Wind People."

There in the far ground on a great flat mountain is a sparkling jewel. The great earthsip of the Windpeople grows larger and larger. The Childpersons have never seen anything of such splendor. The sun approaches the turning.

The Journey to Argonon

They find a smooth surface that Rom calls a road. Rows and rows of plantfriends form green blankets over the thirsty earth. At the earlyslopes of the great earthship Argonon, Rom follows the smooth earth into a great hole in the mountain. He talks to the gatekeeper on his communicator.

Lily's eyes and mind can barely see what they see. So much for her eyes and so much for her understanding. They leave the transporter and enter a small room. Steel doors close with a whir. The room whines softly. Lily feels a lifting. Rom looks at the big eyes of the Childpersons, "Do not have fear Childpersons, you will see much you have not known. Enjoy the learning. This is mindtime."

61

The Day of the Heart

THE WAYS OF THE WIND PEOPLE

The steel doors open with a wush. Rom, Ren, Lily, Mark, Morgan and the two elderguides of force see three Greeters before them.

Good Welcome! says the greeter in the center as he bows from his waist. "I am Arman, this is Ruel, and … "

"I am Og," speaks the one on the left.

They step out and sign the universal greeting. "We are full of great regard to be in the great place of living of the People of the Wind," speaks Rom. "I have brought Ren, 3 Childpersons, and 2 elderguides to see your way of living. And I am Rom the Elderguide of Earth and Sky from Theta 3 of the Valley of Memories. We have come to bring you Ren, who would like to live with the Wind People as one of you."

Arman raises his hand and signs that this is enough for now.

"There will be a good time to weigh this request. For now, please allow us to show you our Earthship and your rooms for rest."

They walk a few steps and enter a great hall. It is much more than a great hall, it is an inside world with trees and grass and water and flowers. On all sides are many rooms with places of living that open into this inside world. They twinkle like the daynight sky.

Ruel, the greeter, is also the guide. "Our People made this Mesa their home over two hundred years ago. Because this place is the Father of Winds, we made out homes in a great circle. Over the years, the circle grew and grew leaving only the light shafts that you see above you. The Wind People live in this world much of our hours."

Lily listens with all of her heartmind, but so many words she does not know. What are these years? What are hours? She knows she can ask Mark and Morgan later when they have found their place of resting.

☙❧ The Day of the Heart

Ruel walks them to the lake in the inner world.

Lily says to Mark, "The Wind People have made their own valley. And they have made their own sky." There are birds and bees and flowers and rivers that gurgle. There are people everywhere walking and talking. These Wind People group around tables drinking and eating where they laugh and speak loudly. They have bright short robes with big sleeves and pants that tuck into high soft boots. They wear jewels on their fingers, on their arms, and their necks. Their faces are bright and their bodies are lean.

"How many Wind People live on this Earthship?" speaks Rom.

"We number a thousand thousand," reponds Ruel.

"And your nourishment?"

"Much of our food grows on the outside. Most berries and nuts and fruits live in the innerworld. There are three circles that surround us on the outside. In the Alpha Lands we have our vegetables. In the Beta Lands we grow the grains for our breads, rice and soy beans. In the Theta Lands live our cattle, our sheep, and our fibers. Beyond that is the wilderness that you passed through on your journey. In the wilderness we find many medicines from the cactus. We also take power from our great winds on the Mesas that arise in the wilderness."

Ren speaks to Rom with words close to her body, "These People have made a paradise out of this desert. And you are right about their style. I think they even have fun."

Lily hears Ren's words. "What is fun?"

"Well," says Ren, "it is the opposite of Work. No, it is play. Do you know the word play."

"I think Mark and Morgan and I play in our freetime."

"Well that is what fun is," says Ren.

The Ways of the Wind People

Rom looks at Ren and signs to the Childpersons to hold their tongues.

Ruel guides the visitors into a tunnel. The walls are painted yet they glow like the lightflies. They walk for a short while and come to a gray steel door. The Father of Winds sleeps in the morning. This is a good time to go outside. Ruel pushes a big red button on the side of the wall. The doors open like the room that moves. Whush! There before them is a view like nothing Lily has ever seen. It is more grand than the view from the heights of the Mountain of Hope. Before them lies a lake of green with small paths and small streams. Towards the turning is a great lake of royal blue water.

"We raise our fish in the Lake of the East," says Ruel.

Ren gazes off into the horizon. "What is that flashing I see on that Mesa?"

"Those are the wind fields where we take the gifts of the Father of Winds."

"But I see them turning? And there is no wind here."

"Yes, father wind is awaking, and soon he will be here. But we have some time."

Outside, they walk on grass that is cut as short as the hair of a childone. Many Wind People are walking and talking and running and tending their gardens. Many are sitting and laying on chairs that look more like places of daynightrest. They barely have clothes on their bodies. They are facing the turning and bathing in the early sun. They pay no attention to the travelers.

"What are they doing?" asks Morgan.

"They are sun bathing." says Ren.

"Why" says Mark.

"So they can have a good tan." says Ren. "I think I'm going to like this place."

☙ The Day of the Heart

They walk for long while around the outside. The air is cool, and it is fresh.

"The Father comes, we should go inside," says Ruel. I will show you to your quarters so you may rest. There will be food in your cabinets. Rom, I will come when the time of discussion is set. Until then, be our guests and enjoy the Great Earthship."

Ruel guides the travelers inside and down a hallway. It is lined with doors. The walls and the celling glow.

"Who would stay with their sleeping room facing the life of the inner world? And who wishes see out to the outerworld? Remember the Wind."

Ren chooses in, as do the childones. Rom and the Elderguides choose the rooms facing the outerworld.

Rom sees that everyone is with comfort, and finds his place.

The room is small but well lit. A place of sleeping folds down out of the wall. He rests from the long journey. His heartmind is full as his dreamworld rushes in and the Father of Winds awakes.

The Ways of the Wind People 〰

The Day of the Heart

BLACKNESS AT DAYNIGHT

"I think we have something finally Jarlar," reports Achar, Jarlar's Chief of Staff. Apparently, the First Lady went into the Valleys over three days ago. "Our infrared pictures show a ramp up of energy in the Councilmound at Theta Three in the Valley of Memories. That was the first Valley to raise its light force."

"What's the history on that Valley?" asks Jarlar.

"There is no history of insurgency. It's one of the most peaceful of all the Pacts." Echar walks to the front of Jarlar's glass and steel desk and lays the reports on it. "Could be she have gotten lost and then discovered."

"Has there been any attempt at communication?"

"Nothing," says Echar.

Jarlar rubbs his hands down accross his face and twirls his fingers in his short dark beard. "I don't want any word of this leaked. Cancel all events for the First Lady. If someone gets too curious, stonewall them. Then bring them into your confidence and tell them off the record that you think she may be ill. But tell them you really can't confirm that. Send a recon unit into that valley and make sure they dress right. Get Colonel Lowe to lead the operation."

"Any incursion could be a violation of the Treaty," says Echar.

Jarlar coughs and clears his lungs with a growl. "Let me worry about the affairs of State. Lowe knows how to be careful. Tell him to handpick the men out of my personal guard."

As the evening comes, the City lights up. The transporters line the boulevards making them ribbons of light, white on one side and red on the other. Jarlar stands at the large window next to his desk that looks down the main boulevard that leads to the palace.

He thoughts range from anger to concern over the disappearance of his wife. There is a large knock on the large delicately carved doors. It is the official knock of his personal guard.

"Yes," yells Jarlar in a long long tone.

"Mr. President, It is Colonel Lowe"

༄༅། The Day of the Heart

"Send him in."

Colonel Lowe steps briskly into the room, clicks his heels and brings his fist to his chest. "Lowe reporting, Sir."

Jarlar walks from the window. "At ease Colonel. Take a seat." Jarlar gestures with his hands for Lowe to sit at the large war room table in the middle of the office.

"We have a very dicey situation here Colonel. We have indications that the First Lady has been taken hostage by the People of the Sun in the Valley of Memories, Theta 3.

Lowe doesn't move a muscle.

"I want you to go in there tonight with a small company. Disguise yourselves. Find out what you can and report back immediately."

You will have to leave your Levitons on the border. Land here." Jarlar put his finger on the war room map. "Then move on the ground with land bots as quickly as possible to here. The light force has been energized so you will be detected. Find the ... what to you call them?"

"Elderguides," says Lowe.

"Find the Elderguide of the Pact that runs the Council and tell him that you are looking for a missing person. Keep your lasers hidden and don't make a scene."

"Yes, Mr. President." Lowe gets out of the war room chair, walks to the door, turns, salutes, and heads for the secret operations room to meet with the men he has chosen for the job.

Blakness at Daynight

In less than an hour, Jarlar hears the humming of the Levitons and then sees a thin trail of lights arising into the sky as Lowe and his men head for the borderlands of the People. Battle Levitons can fly at speeds that even fool the eye.

Jarlar looks at his watch. Lowe and his men will be there in an hour. With their speed bots, they will be at Theta 3 in two more.

The People of Pact Theta 3 have begun to serve the evening Plates of Nourishment when Lem, the Great Elderguide of Force slips over to the table next to the Elderguides of Mysteries. "We have sensed a disturbance in the lightforce," speaks Lem with a voice close to his body.

The Elderguide looks up from his plate and signs to the other elderguides. The conversations continue, but the Elderguides feel a trouble. By the end of the passing of the plates of nourishment, the Elderguide of Force rises and speaks. "We have visitors arriving. All Elderguides go to your places of concern. All childones, Childpersons, and Motherones, go to your place of safety."

Raiza quickly gathers her things and moves with her Childpersons to their place of safety. In her life with the Pact she have never known such an order from the Great Elderguide of Force.

As the moon reveals itself at the turning, the faint sound of walking is heard on the trail that leads to the Lake of Time.

Some of the Elderguides gather at the Circle of Truth. Others have found their places of concern. The Pact center is quiet.

Lowe and his men appear at the edge of the Pact center.

Lowe speaks," People of Theta 3, we come from the Valley of Long Beginnings. May we enter your place of living?

"Enter in Peace" says Lem.

Lowe and his men come to the edge of the circle and stop.

"We are looking for a lossling. It is a woman who has broken the way. Have you known or heard of such a lossling?"

The Elderguides sign to one another. "We know of a lossling, but she is no longer here. We could not allow her to live with the People. She has made her way out of the valleys," speaks Lem.

"And where has she gone?"

ꙮ The Day of the Heart

Blakness at Daynight ༼༽

"She left 3 suncycles ago to find a place of living with the Wind People." Lem rises and walks to the edge of the circle. "She no longer wishes to be of the People of the Cities. You should let this be."

Lowe looks at Lem and takes a step back. " We are grateful for these words."

"Will you stay in Theta 3? This daynight grows old and the moon grows dark?" asks Lem.

"We go as we cam," says Lowe as he turns and signs to his men to follow. The White Man had come.

The Day of the Heart

OG

Rom awakes with a knock on his door. "Elderguide Rom, the time for discussion is at hand."

The wind outside is howling. Even the tight well fitting windows and the thick masonry walls of the earthship cannot keep Father Wind from making his presence known. Rom informs the Elderguides and Ren that the time for discussion has come. They meet Ruel in the gathering room. The childones will be given an opportunity to join the mindtime of the Wind People's learningones.

Rom, Ren, and the Elderguides, led by Ruel, make their way down the glowing halls back into the inner world of the Earthship. They walk into the place of discussion. The leaders of the Wind People are seated in two long rows on each side of the door. At the other side of the door sits three judges. Rom recognizes the judge in the middle. He is Og.

"Welcome to Argonon and to this place of discussion," says Og.

"We have assembled here today to hear the request of Rom the Elderguide from The Valley of Memories." He has brought a woman who would live with us if it be our pleasure."

"Rom why have you brought this woman to live with us?" asks the judge to the right.

"We found Ren in a hole in the earth on the earlyslopes of the Mountain of Hope. She has left the White Man."

"And why does she not live with the People of the Sun?" says the other judge on the left.

"The People of the Sun live in the way that was given as we left the Tombs many Sunseasons ago. We have, as this woman says, many strange ways. Our life and our ways, though full and joyous, do not share the ways of the White Man. I told Ren of the Wind People and of the Earthship Argonon. I told her how you dress with jewels and in robes of magnificent color and threads, how you drink and eat, and that you accept many humans of many ways."

"And what do think of our ways woman Ren?" asks Og.

༄༅། The Day of the Heart

"I have not been with you a day, yet I find your ways to be somewhat like the ways of the cities that I have left. Your ways seem to make for a happy people. This morning I saw sun bathers. I see many lovely fabrics and shoes. This inner world that you have made is greater than any I have ever seen." Ren walks down between the rows of listeners. "I see faces of wisdom and courage and of peace. That is what I want ... to be wise and courageous and at peace."

"Why have you run from the Cities?" asks Og.

"The cities are not a good place to live. There is much sickness. There are many in the tombs. The air is full of poisons and the life there is without meaning. There is great wealth but there is still great poverty. And we are not free. We must wear transponders that tell our every position and if we do not, we are sent to the tombs."

Og brings his hands down from where they seem to hold up his face. "And what can you offer the Wind People in return?"

Ren looks at the judges then turns around and looks at the two rows of listeners. "I can offer beauty and I can offer my knowledge of the Cities I have left."

"Do you know the sciences or the arts or drama?" says the judge on the right.

"I know that I enjoy them all." Ren looks at Rom and his deep clear eyes. "I know that I cannot go back to the cities."

Og stands from his high position and runs his wise eyes over Rom, Ren, the elderguides and the two rows of listeners. He looks to his left and to his right. "Are there any with more thoughts on this discussion? We will talk among ourselves and give you our answer when we are of one mind."

Ruel escorts Rom, Ren, and the elderguides out of the place of discussion. Ruel returns to the place of discussion.

"What do you think Rom?" asks Ren?

"They will say yes." Rom looks up at the top of the innerworld and sinks deep into his heartmind. Visions run through his mindseye.

Ruel comes out of the place of discussion. "We are of one mind. We will take the woman from the cities."

Og

Ren smiles with relief and lets out a sigh of joy. "Oh thank you, thank you." Rom takes in a long breath and lets it slip slowly back into the air around him. He is happy, but he is sad. He will leave Ren but he will not forget her. He is of two minds.

The Day of the Heart

THE RETURN

Rom walks with Ren in the great inner world of the Wind People. The path leads by green beds of flowers over small creeks that gurgle and splash through the round rocks. At the small bridge that crosses the brook, Rom stops and looks at Ren. "We will leave as the earth finds it shadow."

"I know. I want to thank you."

Ren leans forward and gives Rom a kiss. Rom does not move. "Have you ever been kissed before?"

"Only by the sweet spirits."

"You have never been kissed by a woman?"

Rom looks into the eyes of Ren. "It is not our way."

"Did you like it?"

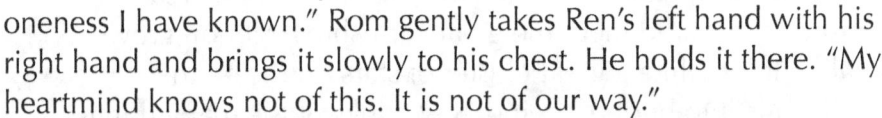

"I find that the soft skin of your cheek gives pleasure to my cheek. It is like sweet food and drink and the pleasure of the oneness I have known." Rom gently takes Ren's left hand with his right hand and brings it slowly to his chest. He holds it there. "My heartmind knows not of this. It is not of our way."

Rom turns and walks from the bridge that crosses the small brook that runs through the inner world. He looks back at Ren who is standing on the bridge. "I will come to this great earthship again." He signs to Ren but it is not the signing for "goodbye," it is the sign for "until the time that comes."

Ren watches as Rom leaves the innerworld and enters the hall that leads to his quarters. She thinks to herself. "I will enjoy my new life here. These people will welcome me. I will make friends and I will find peace here." Yet she can't stop thinking about Rom.

As her gaze flows over the flowers and beauty of the innerworld, she sees Lily running towards her with a great smile and a face full of excitement. "The mind school of the Wind People is nothing like our mind time," she says.

"Did you make any friends?" asks Ren.

꩜ The Day of the Heart

"Yes, I found 3 friends. But Ren, I saw what they call a movie. Have you ever seen a movie?"

"Many. I have even been in some movies."

"Ren, the mindguides have said that I may return. If Raiza and the Pact agree, I will be able to visit you."

"I will look forward to that time Lily." Ren gives Lily a big hug. Lily squeezes Ren and holds her for many breaths. Ren bends down to Lily and places the necklace with the large jewel in her hands. "I know your people do not wear adornments but take this and hide it in your necessaries. Keep it in remembrance of me. Go now Lily," says Ren. A small tear falls from her cheek as she watches Lily disappear into the glowing hall.

Rom, Lily, Mark, Morgan, and the two elderguides of force gather their necessaries and walk to the room that lifts and falls. They arrive at the room where their transporter is waiting. The gateman greets them and helps them load their necessaries.

The day night is awake with stars. The moon is about to reach the turning. As they make their way past the green rows of growing nourishment down the smooth earth Lily now knows as a road, Lily, Mark, and Morgan look back out the rear of the transporter. Behind them the great earthship Argonon grows smaller. It look like a great cluster of stars on the earth.

Lily falls into her heartmind. She thinks of the many things she has seen on this journey. She thinks of Ren. She remembers the mindschool and the friends she made. Images of the great innerworld flow across her mindseye. And the movie? She wonders why her people have no such thing.

They move off the smooth surface and head in the direction of the turning. The moon has lost its full light and wanes as it moves through the daynight sky.

Lily looks back one more time. Argonon is now just a small jewel of light. She will have many memories to share with the other Childpersons of the Pact. She thinks of her Motherone Raiza. She thinks to herself, "It will be nice to be in my place of sleeping."

Rom guides the transporter swiftly. "We will make our way directly," he declares. "We will arrive in the valleys by the late

The Return

early day of the next sun cycle. When the moon reveals itself next at the turning we will find Theta 3."

Lily wonders why Rom hurries so.

The Day of the Heart

THE BETRAYAL

Ren looks out over the innerworld of the earthship from the large balcony of her new place of living on level 20. Down below her, the Wind People look very small. Above her is a lensed skylight. During the day, light pours through it down to the innerworld. At night, it becomes a soft yet powerful sun. In the inner world night never comes.

There is a large picture screen in her living room and a smaller one in her bedroom. All of the walls and ceilings glow with a golden hue that makes her skin look rich and healthy. Her bathing room is full of mirrors. She has not even seen herself since she left the Cities for her nature trip except for the reflection she saw in the small pool that gathers water from the spring in the upper meadow below the oak circle.

She sits down at the vanity and opens the mirror door. Inside there is a rich assortment of perfumes, skin lotions, brushes for her hair, and tools for cleaning her teeth. *These People treat me as a Queen*, she thinks.

She looks deep into her reflection in the mirror ... deep into her own soul. She remembers when she would spend hours and hours preparing herself before she appeared with Jarlar for a special Dinner of State. She remembers how they met at the set of the movie she last starred in. She was waiting for the director to bring her on to the set and there was a knock on the door. She turned and in walked a dashing man in a well tailored military suit with golden epaulets on his shoulders. He carried 2 dozen red roses. He bowed and introduced himself as Jarlar. Although she cared nothing about politics even she knew who this man was. He was the leader of the Cities! He has the title of President, but he had been a general. He was the general that had won the wars with the Cities of the East and of the South. He had triumphed over all of the world of the Cities. He was never elected. He was proclaimed president by the World Senate.

The first time she met Jarlar, he was charming and delightful. He spoke of her work as an actress and how much he enjoyed it. He spoke of the importance of her work and of the value of stories

৩৯ The Day of the Heart

told in light and sound. During their first dinner together she was amazed with his knowledge of art and literature. When he asked her to marry him, she was taken by his presence. He was a strong man with many talents. And he was powerful!

When she became the first lady, she lived as a Queen in his palace. She had servants and assistants. She had not cooked a meal since she was a girl living with her mother in the lower east side of the City. All that seemed like a very long time ago.

She looked at the small lines around her eyes. She was not so young. Still, with a little make up here and little there she could look like a beautiful young woman. *Perhaps I will be able to go back to the movies, the Wind People know much of stories in light and sound*, she thought.

There is a chime from her door. "Yes?"

"Ren, this is Ruel. You are to come with me."

"Why?"

"You are to meet with Og."

Ren puts a little make up on her face and powders her forehead and nose. She runs a brush through her dark brown hair. "You must give me just a moment." She is not accustomed to interruptions of her private time but she thinks to herself, *I cannot keep Og waiting, he has been so generous in allowing me to stay and the quarters they have provided for me are as nice as any I have known.*

Ruel and Ren walk down the glowing halls to the elevator.

"Where are we going," asks Ren.

"We are to meet Og in his private chamber," answers Ruel.

They exit the elevator and walk through the innerworld into a section of the earthship where there are more doors and even higher ceilings than the ones in her new home.

Ruel shows her the door to Og's private chamber. Ren knocks, and the door opens. "You called for me Og?"

"Yes, please come in. May I offer you something to drink?"

Og sits at a white desk in a great chair of white fabric.

"You have come a long way," says Og as he moves around the desk. "Your time with the People of the Sun, was it profitable?" Og gestures for Ren to sit in the chair next to the couch and places a

The Betrayal

glass of wine on the table in front.

Ren sits. "What do you mean Og? Most of the time I hid in a cave drinking water from a small spring, eating berries and honey."

"But surely you had some reason to be among them."

"I knew nothing about the people except what we are taught in the Cities." Ren takes a sip out of the wine. This is very good, do you grow the grapes yourselves?"

"We provide for all of our needs." Og takes a breath and look directly at Ren. "So you ran away from the Cities because the life there was not to your liking?"

"I ran away because I was not free." Ren takes another sip of the wine and leans back into the large overstuffed chair. "There are many problems in the Cities and the Ruler, the man named Jarlar, rules with his fist and not his heart. He has put many of his citizens in the Tombs. We must all wear transponders or be sent to the Tombs. Jarlar knows of your presence at all times. It is a life of fear." Ren takes another sip of the wine and sinks deeper into the soft fabric of the chair. Her mind begins to whirl and her eyes become dim. In the wall behind the desk, she hears the whush of a door. Her eyes grow dimmer.

In the dim light of fading consciousness she sees a man standing in the doorway. He is in a dark suit with golden epaulets on his shoulders.

It is Jarlar.

The Day of the Heart

ROM THE ELK

Rom, Lily, Mark, Morgan, and the Two Elderguides of Force arrive at Theta 3 as the half moon reveals itself at the turning. They are tired from the long journey from Argonon to the Valley of Memories. Lily is glad to be home. She had never been away from her Motherone for even one suncycle. She has been away from Raiza for 5 suncycles.

Rom and the two elderguides make their way to the Councilmound where the Great Elderguide of Force awaits. "The White Man came on the daynight of your leaving in disguise as the People." The Great Elderguide looks into the sky and then he looks to the earth. "They said they were looking for a lossling. We told them we had seen such a lossling and that she was no longer here."

Rom feels a sorrow in his heartmind. "And you told them?"

"We told them she had gone to find a place of living with the Wind People," says the Great Elderguide. "Rom, why would the White Man risk breaking the Treaty over one woman lossling?"

Rom rubs his mouth with his hands and then rubs his forehead. "That means Ren is no longer in Argonon. If the White Man knows that she has warned us, they will kill her. Or they will throw her deep into the Tombs. If they know that she warned us, they may come with force even sooner. Or, perhaps they will not come at all. Have we had any more disturbance in the light force?"

"Not since the daynight of their coming," says the Great Elderguide. The other Great Elderguides begin to enter the Councilmound. They have grave heartminds. This time that is coming will be like no other they have known. One by one they take their places on their colored mats. The Elderguide of Mysteries begins the Judgment Time. "The other Councils are of one mind. They too believe that the woman speaks a truth, they too believe that she hides another."

"And what is their judgment?"

"All the Councils agree. Rom, you will lead us for this time. It is your heartwork," says the Great Elderguide of Mysteries. "We will await your judgment." The Great Elderguide stands and puts a necklace with a large clear stone around Rom's neck. It bears

ಅ The Day of the Heart

the crystal of caring and the heart of the people. "You will be our defender, our hope, you will be Rom the Elk"

Rom leaves the Mound and makes his way to the great jutting rock, his place of awareness. How will he defend the People of the Sun from Jarlar? Why did Jarlar send his men into the valleys to find Ren? Who is this Ren who has run from the Cities? Has she now found death or is she in Jarlar's Tombs?

Rom sits under the great rock as he did as a child. He brings these mysteries into his heartmind. He grabs the rich earth with both hands and smells of it. He can smell the hint of Ren. He makes himself quiet. His breath finds a new slowness. He looks over the mountain into the stars. The daynight is bright from the light of the half moon. When the turning brings the moon to the top of the heavens, the sun will reveal itself at the turning.

The trees are aglow. The late daynight cooling brings small drops of water to each leaf and blade of grass. They sparkle and glow in the light of moon. A night owl flies by and rest in a great living Oak. Rom breathes deeper and more slowly. There is not a whisper of Father Wind. The daynight is silent.

His being rises. Up, up, above the trees and the great rock below. Riding on the oneness, he flies over the valleys, and the Lake of Time. He travels like the eagle over time and space. His being sees the Cities and a palace below. A balcony stands over a great road of light that leads to the palace. Light flows out of the glass doors. The light calls his being into a great room. There is the voice of man. The words bring Rom closer. In the eye of his being he sees a man standing in the doorway. He wears a dark suit with golden epaulets on his shoulders. It is Jarlar.

On a golden place of sleeping lies a woman. Her hair is tangled. Her eyes are like blood and they weep from great sorrow. Her clothes look like flags worn by the wind. Rom has found Ren!

Rom's being flies on the oneness to a great lamp with many crystals.

"What was that?" says Jarlar.

"What was what?" says Ren.

"That tinkling, see the crystal on the chandelier is moving ever so slightly? " Jarlar walks to the light and stills the moving crystal.

"It was only the wind," says Ren, "only the wind."

Rom the Elk 🙦

The Day of the Heart

THE WISDOM OF EVIL

"Did you find your time in the Tombs to be to your liking my sweet princess?"

Jarlar walks and sits on the edge of the great golden bed and touches Ren with his thumb to her forehead. "I have been thinking. What to do … what to do. If I simply put you to death, it would be quite an embarrassment for me. Of course, I would make your death look like an accident. You could accidentally be hit by a speeding transporter. No, that would be too messy and who knows, you might live. Oh you would likely be paralyzed and your pretty face would be ruined. Such a pity.

"Or, one of my enemies could try to kill me and instead gun you down. That could be quite useful. The citizenry would feel quite sorry for me. But that would be too fast. You would not suffer enough to satisfy the wrong you have wrought." Jarlar gets up from the bed.

"It is one thing to have enemies, but an enemy in my own bed. You were a second rate actress with second rate talents, and a reputation of the street and I lifted you up to be my wife and made you first lady of the World."

Jarlar turns violently, "Why?"

"Why, my pretty Ren, why did you disgrace me and commit treason? I have given you everything."

Ren rises from the golden bed. "You did not give me love."

"Bah … who needs love when you have power. Besides I gave you lots of love. It was you who held back your love."

"There was no love Jarlar. You love power, nothing else. I was your trophy, not your love."

"Enough, enough. It doesn't matter anymore. What matters is what to do with you." Jarlar stares out the balcony door down the long avenue of lights. "I could put you in the Tombs I suppose. You could live in the dark eating canned food and germ filled water until you died an early death. I could tell the Newspaper that you were kidnapped by the People in the Valleys. That would give me a good excuse to break the Treaty."

"Even your newspaper would never believe that Jarlar. The

ಌ **The Day of the Heart**

People of the Sun are hopelessly nonviolent. They have no weapons, no transportation. My god they don't even have roads. They walk around all day worshipping the earth and the sky. Their children have no malice in their hearts. They are a beautiful people. Maybe a little goofy."

Jarlar turns and looks back at his wife. "I could say the Wind People stole you."

"Right. The Wind People have powers that we even don't understand. They would destroy you."

'Not if I hit them first."

Ren holds her breath and stares at Jarlar. "And you wonder why I don't love you."

Jarlar walks back toward the golden bed. "No I think a quick death would be too good for you. And the Tombs, though quite effective in dealing out pain, would allow you too much quiet time. I think the best way to manage this problem is simply to keep you with me under house arrest. You will be my wife when I need your pretty face. You will be seen with me in formal events. You will smile and you will wear your jewels and your gowns and your shoes and you will come to me when I say come."

Jarlar suddenly stops. "The amulet that I gave you ... where is it?"

"I lost it."

Jarlar anxiously leans down to Ren and grabs her hair. "Where did you lose it?"

"I don't know. What are you going to do? Kill me?"

Jarlar releases his grip on Ren's long brown hair and storms to the bottom of the bed. He stares at Ren with a look that even she has never seen. "No, I'm not going to kill you. I'm going to make you watch me kill whoever I must kill to get it back. If you know where it is, you will tell me. If you don't, you will have the misfortune of watching me find it."

"Guard," yells Jarlar. "Take the First Lady to her new accommodations. And see that she takes her medicine. She has not been feeling well lately."

The Wisdom of Evil

Jarlar watches as Ren is taken away through the door. He is fuming. He lights a cigarette and walks to the balcony. He doesn't hear the small tinkling of the moving crystal on the chandelier. It is almost dawn.

✺ The Day of the Heart

MADERA

Rom returns to his body at the great jutting rock as the sun reveals itself at the turning. As his earthform awakes, he sees the brown owl. "Thank you wisefriend for watching my earthform while I journeyed on the oneness." The owl blinks twice and flies into the deep forest.

Rom has not rested his daymind for two suncycles. He is tired yet alert. Full yet empty. There is much to be done.

On his way from his place of awareness, he sees Lily on her way to her mid circle. "Good new day Lily Childperson. Have you rested well from our journey?"

"My Motherone missed me more than I missed her I think."

"As it should be," says Rom.

Rom makes his way to the Councilmound. "My being has been in the Cities this daynight. I know our enemy and I know his heart. We must prepare for his coming. I go to Madera to speak of my knowings."

Madera is the Queen Motherone of all of the Pacts. Her place of living is in the Valley of Joy. She is the oldest of the oldest. Her Motherone came out of the Tombs. She lives in a tree that is older than the People. Although she cannot speak, her ears still have life and her heartmind is full.

"We have a great trouble" signs Rom with his hands.

"Speak with your voice, and I will sign," signs Madera.

"The White Man comes, we must prepare."

"And why will they break the Treaty?" signs Madera.

"They have a leader named Jarlar," says Rom. "He understands not. He keeps his wife under lock and key, he speaks of great violence, and he has lost an amulet."

"He understands more than you know." signs Madera. "This is a great trouble. My mother spoke of this time when I was a childone. There is a key and this key is held by a childone. Rom, you are courageous and your heartmind is clear. You will know. You must practice the Sun Man Moon. This is my story and for you I have waited for many season cycles. You will ride the oneness. But you must have the key."

༄༅ The Day of the Heart

With these signs, Madera, the oldest of the oldest, slumps just a little in her chair and her spirit passes. The heart of the tree trembles as her spirit rises. The ground grumbles, Father Wind rises up. It is as if the turning stops for just a moment. The Great Motherone of the People has walked through the door of the otherworld.

Rom remembers every sign. He has need of mindrest. Yet he must pursue his heartwork. The Greatcouncil must hear of his knowings. They must learn of his plan to deal with this trouble.

Each Pact sends one elderguide to the Greatcouncil. Only once have they met, when the time of trouble with the Wind People arose. They meet in a field where the grass grows high and the sky is wide. Their number is many thousands. They cover the meadow. In the center is a grass mound. Not one has ever seen so many of the People in one place.

Rom looks over the great field of the People. It is a blanket of grays and browns of every hue. His heartmind feels joy yet his face is like stone. There is much speaking and signing. The sounds roll across the field into the forest like the slow thunder of the rainstorm. Rom rises and makes his way to the top of the grass mound. The thunder of the toungespeaking begins to grow weak.

The earth finds its shadow as daynight approaches.

Rom faces the turning and signs to the times that will come. He raises his hands and signs to the Sky. He looks down at the earth and praises the trees and the flowers and all living things. He raises his hands and cries out a song. "Ooooooooooooooom," he sings in strong low voice. The People join in his song. "Ooooooooooooooooom" they sing in different tones. The song grows louder and more beautiful. The sound makes a wave of earthlight that moves through the gathering vibrating the being of each elderguide. The wave enters the head and descends down the spine, then it turns up to the chest where it enlivens the heart. As the wave grows, the song grows. As the song grows, the wave grows. Then, new tones are heard. They are lower than the lowest and higher than the highest.

Rom stands tall holding the Crystal of the People high with both hands. The wave of earthlight rises from the hearts of the

Madera

thousands on the meadow and moves to the mound where Rom the Elk stands. The earthlight wave begins to sparkle like the daynight sky. The sparkling enters the Crystal. The crystal begins to glow ... brighter and brighter and brighter as the sparkling pours in. Rom and the thousands sing like the thunder.

Rom takes the white light crystal and places it on a tall pole.

The great harmonic thunder stops with a wave of his hands. The crystal makes the daynight as day. Every face is bathed in its warm clear light. Rom's face glows bright as the sun.

"This day is of the People," speaks Rom in a voice he has not known. "We are of the Oneness. We are of the Sun."

A great roar arises that deafens the ears. Rom waves his hands and the roar grows weak in one breath.

"Our Valleys will be made high. Our time is come! Our White Heart will guide us through the darkness ahead. Be here now with your heartminds and honor this place."

Rom turns and signs to 12 Elderguides of Passage. They bring the earthform of Madera, the Queen of the Pacts, the Motherone of Motherones, up to the top of the mound. They place her earthform on a high platform of wood. The white light crystal stands above her. She begins to glow. Her earth form becomes like glass. Then in a twinkling, her earth form is no more.

"Her time has passed, a new time is born," speaks Rom. "Stay with me this daynight in the light of the white heart. When the giving moon reaches the turning, find sleep on the meadow. When the sun reveals itself at the turning, we will be of one mind. Our way will be clear and our path will be bright."

With these words, Rom climbs up to the platform where Madera had been. He goes into nightsleep. The white light crystal bathes his body in light. The meadow is quiet. The People are one.

༄༅ The Day of the Heart

PREPARATIONS

"Jarlar, Your forces are ready."
Jarlar is sitting in the supreme commanders chair positioned at the head of a large square table in the war room. The war room is in a secret bunker close to the palace. He is surrounded by his generals. To his left are the generals of the land and of the sea. To his right are the generals of the air and of space. On the other side of the table sit the strategist, the technical specialist, and the communication specialist. Behind them is a large screen that displays any map or view at any scale. From here, the whole earth can be viewed. Cameras from space send images to the war room computers where they can be enhanced and magnified.

The half moon is rising in the dark polluted sky.

"We have indications that a large gathering of the People of the Sun is occurring here," says the General of Space. "It's the largest gathering we have ever seen. They have amassed a large force here, a map of the valleys in the Valley of Joy shows on the screen. We have also found an energy emission that is coming out of the valley. This may be some new weapon that they developed."

"We can move our initial ground forces to here with Levitons and bring the support with troop tranporters to here. Since there are no roads, they will be a little slow in getting there."

"How long?" says Jarlar.

"One maybe two days," says the General of the land.

"I imagine we could have the entire theater under our control within 48 hours after that."

"If we believe this new weapon is a threat, we can send our strikers in and take it now," says the General of Space.

"In all due respects Mr. President this is not going to be much of a war. The People of the Sun have been totally nonviolent for many generations. They don't know how to fight. The biggest job will be rounding them all up and keeping them fed."

Jarlar rises and puts both hands on the table. He looks at his generals "We're not going to that. The Wind People will track our movements and see that we are breaking the Treaty and they

೧೦ The Day of the Heart

will attack us well before we can finish the People of Sun off. We might as well start where we will need to finish."

The generals look at each other with serious faces. "Mr. President, the Wind People have some pretty serious capabilities. Our knowledge of their weaponry is almost nil. Argonon is fortified to withstand anything we can hit them with. They can knock out every striker from space and anything else we put in the air," says the General of the Air.

"That's right, but their power supplies are more vulnerable and their food supplies even more so. Besides, it is the Wind People who have brought this on themselves. It was they who kidnapped the first lady and it was they who traded her for my promise to keep the peace. They must be taken out, then the People of the Sun will be helpless. Once we have the Wind People's weapons, there will be no force on earth than can oppose us."

Jarlar stands in front of the large screen. "We bring in everything we have in on levitons and surround the earthship. At the same time I want all of our strikers to attack here and here and here. That will knock out their power leaving them only with their backups. That will reduce their laser cannon capabilities. If we hit them all at once, with no warning, we can cripple them. They won't even have their light shields activated."

"If we have to we will do it the old fashion way. We will surround them until they have no more food and no more energy." Jarlar looks at his generals. They are silent. "Any question?"

"Are there not protections that were put in the Treaty that protect us all?" asks the General of Space.

"We will need no protection from others. We will be the most powerful force on the Earth. There will be no City, no People of any kind who would dare challenge our rule."

Once we have brought the Wind People to hunger, they will be forced to agree to our terms. Then, the People of the Sun and their valleys will be ours. We can put our poisons far away from us in the wilderness of the Wind People. Our Citizens will stop getting sick. We can extend our roads into the valleys and make the land useful. Those who need clean air will find it there."

"The citizens of the Cities will praise us for our boldness, they

Preparations

will write songs of our strength. The earth will again be united ... under our flag. This is our destiny."

Jarlar leans on the table and looks at each of his generals. "And, each of you will meet glory and each of you will become very very rich. That is my word."

ꙮ The Day of the Heart

THE ATTACK

The early dawn begins to break the darkness over the Wind City. The Moon is in the eastern sky. It seems to be laughing. There are thousands and thousands of Levitons hovering over the City like a great colony of bats. Each Leviton carries 40 robotic shock troopers and six laser cannons. Powered by the power of poisonous burning rocks, they travel faster than sound without making a sound. Their round saucer like forms made of black ceramic alloys make the light shields of the Wind People blind.

The general of space predetermines the targets for each of his strikers. They will stream out of space like a meteor shower. They will strike when the Levitons are in place.

Jarlar stands at the balcony that overlooks the great avenue of lights. In the dim light of early morning, he gives the command.

"Are we ready to go?"

"Yes," says Echar.

"Then go."

The black hovering cloud of Levitons moves towards the darkness like a swarm. At they speed away, they will travel faster than the turning of the earth. It will be darker at Argonon when they arrive than it is now as they leave.

Jarlar is dressed in his war clothes. His boots lace up high on his calf. His black pants tuck neatly into the tops of the boot leaving a stylish flair. They are trimmed in gold. His waistcoat has gleaming golden buttons, the pockets have a fine trim of red. His epaulets make his shoulders broad. The turned up red trimmed collar runs high on his neck. He looks in the mirror and adjusts his cap. He is ready for this day.

Jarlar walks briskly out of his office of state. The Palace Guards give him a smart salute with their hands up and back to the chest. He steps to the open ground outside of the palace to enter his presidential air ship. He stops and tells Echar. "Move the first lady to the Tombs, but leave her an image communicator. I don't want her to miss this. If she has something she wants to say to me, put her through to me."

❧ The Day of the Heart

Jarlar boards the presidential Leviton One. In it is a war room, the presidential quarters, and room for his staff. The other generals will stay at the war room in the bunker. Jarlar must be where the action is.

In less than an hour, the Levitons are in place, and the General of Space has his satellites in place.

"Og, wake up, Og, our light force has detected a massing of satellites in our quadrant," says Ruel.

"Are the EMASERS activated?" says Og.

"They are on half power, we need sunlight to bring them to full charge. I think we are being attacked."

"That cannot be possible. Jarlar and I made a deal for the return of his wife." Og is wrestling with his clothes and racing to his communication station. He pulls up the screen showing the cluster of satellites. He gives the command to shoot the satellites down with the laser cannons. The communicator responds, "This request needs an access code." He quickly types it in.

"Launch the strikers" orders the General of Space.

"Move the Levitons in," orders the General of the Air.

"Energize the shocktroopers" says the General of the Land.

The strikers stream from their perches from the black void of space. They hit their targets and devastate the wilderness. The Levitons move in quickly and secure the ground around the great earthship.

Og looks out from his window and sees black clouds rising from the energy fields in the dim dawn of early morning. The warning lights are flashing and the attack sirens are wailing. The explosions in the distance project bright flashes of orange light on to the walls.

Down below, Og sees the shocktroopers disembarking from the Levitons. They have surrounded the earthship on all sides. They have control of the food, the water, and the energy to power the great earthship. Og rubs his eyes, hoping that this is some bad dream. It is not a dream. It is his worst nightmare.

Jarlar has delivered his terrible might on the Great Earthship Argonon. From the Presidential leviton, Jarlar grins as he looks at the war screen, " The Wind People are mine."

The Attack

The Day of the Heart

THE DOOR OF DESTRUCTION

The silvery edge of the sun greets the turning. Rom awakes from his daynightsleep. His heartmind is full. The Great Council Elderguide of Force, Morel, is waiting for him as comes down from the place of sleeping. The Crystal Heart of the People is glowing like a second sun.

"Jarlar has attacked the Wind People," says Rom.

"I was coming to speak of this," says Morel.

One by one, the still blanket of the People on the meadow comes to life. The word of Jarlar's attack spreads through the gathering like a deep dye in a pool. The earlyday quiet gives way to the talk of many. It grows into a din of fear and concern.

Rom watches from the mound. His eyes are like the Sun.

His long brown hair glistens as it waves in the soft breaths of Father Wind.

"People of the Sun," he says in his new found clear deep voice. "Jarlar has attacked the Wind People with all of his might. Who of us would know his mind? Who of us would place our People in the caring of the Wind People? We have the Crystal Heart of the People. Do we not feel and see its strength?" Rom grabs the pole which holds the great streaming sphere of light and holds it high for the great gathering to see.

The gathering grows hush.

"Go back to your valleys and tell your people of this day. Tell of the lighting of the Crystal Heart of the People. Tell of the victory of life over death. Tell of our Queen Mother, the Motherone of Motherones, and how her earthform was changed out of this world. Tell your Elderguides, your Motherones, and your Childpersons that the People will not fear the White Man. Take of this *Light* and take it to your valleys. Take of this *Light* for it is the Heart of the People. Make this *Light* shine in your own places of living. The darkness cannot withstand the *Light*. If the *Light* opposes the darkness, the darkness grows in its power. Face the *Light* and know not the dark. Go to your Pacts and share this great

༄༅། The Day of the Heart

mystery. Go to your Pacts and live the Way that was given as we were led out of the Tombs. Be here now of the Oneness."

Rom takes the pole with that Greatsphere of Light, and holds it close to the earth. He walks from the Mound and steps slowly with it through the great gathering. "Gaze on it and touch of it so you may know it in your heartmind."

As he walks, the People part from it like water from steep rock. Rom continues walking with white *Light* streaming crystal. "Who will be the first to gaze and to touch?"

An old elderguide of the Valley of Big Trees walks forward. It is the Great Council Elderguide of Mystery. He holds his wrinkled frail hands out with his palms towards the heavens. Rom walks forward to him and gently places the *Light* streaming crystal into both of his hands. He slowly closes his hands over them. The *Light* streams between his fingers showing his bones and his veins.

There is silence. Then the great elderguide speaks in a deep clear voice, "Though White hot, it is cool. Though its *Light* is like the sun, my eyes are blinded not." The Great Council Elderguide of Mystery raises his hands to the gathering and says, "Come and take of this mystery and drink of its *Light*." One by one, each of the thousands files by the *Light* streaming crystal heart. There are no words of the tongue, only signs.

Rom the Elk stands on the Mound as the thousand pass by. He gazes into each of their eyes. He signs to each of them. His hands move from his heart then out, back to the heart and to the sky. It is the sign of Sun Man Moon. When he sees that their eyes have taken of the Sun, he signs for them to stand with him on the mound.

When each has finished, they prepare their necessaries and make ready for the journey back to their Pact. By the late early day, the green grass meadow in the Valley of Joy is as it was. Rom stands on the mound with the ones that have taken the sun unto their eyes. Their number is 12. Together they place the pole back pointing into the heavens. The white *Light* streaming crystal of the heart of the People will live on the mound in the green grass meadow of the Valley of Hope.

The giving moon reaches the falling in the late light of day. The

The Door of Destruction

crystal heart of the People is streaming. This place will know not darkness.

Rom and the twelve elderguides go into the mound. The Childpersons of Alpha 1 bring them their plates of nourishment. They will take of their plates of nourishment and seek their place of wisdom. They have been chosen.

The door of darkness is before them.

109

The Day of the Heart

THE KEY

Lily prepares her place of nightsleep. She finds her bag of necessaries that she took with her on her journey to Argonon. It has only been 3 suncycles since she was there, yet it seems like a like a full moon cycle. She remembers the great earthship and its great innerworld. She remembers her last closeness with Ren and their parting and the amulet that Ren gave her. She leaps up and rummages through her the bag. There lies the beautiful crystal amulet that Ren gave her. She has not spoken of it to anyone, not even her Motherone Raiza. She puts it on her neck and thinks without voicing, "I will wear this during my night sleep so I may be close to Ren."

She falls into nightsleep. Her dreamworld washes across her mindseye. She sees a white stallion with wings flying high in the clouds in the distant sky. The white winged stallion comes closer and closer. Riding on the stallion is a woman.

It is Ren.

"It is good that you sent for me sweet Lily," say Ren. "Come fly with me and I will show you my world. They fly off together on the white winged horse into the heavens. The sky is a rich dark blue and the clouds roll by as great puffy pillows. Out of the blue, a great black cloud appears. The zig-zag lightning lives in it. Out of the black cloud with the zigzag lightning a fire breathing dragon arises. It comes toward them breathing fire and smoke from both of its nostrils. The horse rears up in fear. Ren is thrown into the air and falls. Lily feels great fear. The black dragon opens its mouth to devour Lily and the white winged horse. As the dragon's mouth gets closer and closer, Lily thinks of Rom and the amulet. With a blast of light, the white crystal amulet awakes and blinds the dragon. With another blast of light it separates the black firebreathing dragon from its wings and the dragon falls down, down into a burning lake of fire.

Lily awakes from her nightsleep and jumps out of her place of sleeping. Her forehead and hands are wet. Her legs shake.

Her breath runs. The amulet on her chest is humming like a bee and it has the soft glow of the firefly.

The Day of the Heart

I must tell Rom of my dream and of this crystal amulet, she thinks without voicing. It is mid daynight. How will she get to the Valley of Hope to find Rom? She walks in to the Room of her Motherones's place of sleeping. "Motherone, I have had a strange dream."

"Was it a daynightmare?" says Raiza.

"It was more like a vision," says Lily.

Raiza turns over in her place of sleeping and brings her hand to her forehead. "Go back to your place and we will speak of it when the sun reaches the turning?"

"I must speak of it now," says Lily.

"At the turning sweet childone, at the turning."

Lily goes back to her place of sleeping. She looks out the window at the Turning Star. She must let Rom know of her dream and of the amulet. Her heartmind will not let go of this vision for even a breath. As she lies in her place of sleeping staring at the stars through the star window above her, she hears the faint Beep Beep of her communicator. She answers it.

"Lily, this is Mark, my mind will not rest, are you awake?"

"Yes."

Mark gets very close to the image screen and whispers, "My thoughts will not stop. I can only think of Ren and of Rom."

A thought finds a place in Lily's heartmind. "Mark, I must go to the Valley of Joy this daynight. Can you drive the transporter?"

"I am sure of it," says Mark. "But we cannot use of it without the blessing of an elderguide."

"Rom would give his blessing but he is in the great councilmound. We must make our way now." Mark thinks without voicing for a breath or two. "I will come on the scooter. Meet me at the transporter."

Lily grabs her necessaries and slips out of her place of living. Raiza is deep in nightsleep. Mark arrives. "We may have many elderguide walks of straighttalking for this."

Mark jumps into the cockpit and adjusts the position so his feet can feel the controls on the floor. He pushes the activator button in the way he had seen Rom do. They steal away silently in the latemiddaynight.

"Why are we doing this?" says Mark.

Lily goes through her bag of necessaries, "Because of a dream and because of this." She holds up the amulet. "We must take this to Rom. It is the Key."

The Day of the Heart

THE RETURN TO THE TOMBS

Lily and Mark arrive at the Valley of Hope just as the almost given moon reaches the Turning. The dim light of day is following soon. They had seen the streaming *Light* of the crystal heart of the People from many valleys away. It led them to the green meadow and to the great councilmound.

As they come closer, the streaming *Light* falls onto their faces like the light of day. All around, the trees and the flowers and the grass are alive with color like they have never seen. They get out of the transporter and marvel at the meadow. They can feel the *Light* as it enters their heads, falls down to their spine, and arises to the heart. "This place will be remembered by the People for many generations." says Mark.

"I feel courage and I feel fear," speaks Lily. "I have not known such a feeling before." They walk together hand and hand through the *Light* washed grass slowly. The great council mound is before them. Rom arises from the inside of the Mound and stands with his arms crossed.

"Lily Childperson, your courage has overcome your wisdom. What knowledge has made you so brave?"

"I have had a vision Rom."

Rom unfolds his hands and holds them out. Lily runs to him and hugs him for many breaths. Lily reaches into her bag. "Ren gave me this when we departed from Argonon. This daynight before my nightsleep, I took it from my bag of necessaries and wore it on my heart. Ren came to me on a great white winged horse and on it we rode through the heavens. Then a great dragon appeared out of a black cloud with the zig-zag lightning. The dragon tried to devour us and this amulet sent out a great blast of *Light* that blinded the dragon and cut off its wings."

Rom's bright eyes look down at Lily. "You have done well Lily Childperson to bring me your vision and the amulet."

"Do you know what the dream means?" asks Lily.

ᗩᗰ The Day of the Heart

Rom carefully caresses Lily's forehead. "I know that you have brought the Key."

"The Key to what?"

Rom takes the amulet from Lily and puts it in his journey bag. "We shall know soon enough." Rom walks to the door that leads to the mound, and stops. "You and Mark go to Alpha 1 and communicate with your Motherones. Tell them you have done the heartwork of the People; that Rom has said you have done well. The elderguides will take you to Theta 3."

Lily's ears hear Rom's words but her heartmind does not. "But I want to go with you."

"You cannot go where I go. Make your way to Alpha 1." Rom descends into the mound. Lily stands and watches. A tear slips down to her cheek. She turns and begins to walk to Alpha 1.

"Lily! You and Mark make your place in Alpha 1. When the moon is in the sun, you will again see Ren." Lily's face changes into Joy. Rom signs *Good Journey* and descends into the mound again.

As Rom enters the Mound, the 12 chosen ones await his words.

"Six will go with me into darkness, six will arrive in Glory. Who of you chooses darkness?" Rom hands each of them a seed and a small flower. Rom collects the secret choice of each chosen elderguide and puts them in the small journey bag. He looks into the bag. There are six seeds and six flowers. "Those who are seed come with me for the planting. Those who arrive in Glory must remain in the mound in their place of wisdom. When the moon is in the sun, leave this place of council and follow our path. And bring the two Childpersons, they are indeed bright flowers."

Rom and the Six ascend from the Mound. The sun has reached the turning. The almostgiven moon stands above it. Their faces are aglow with the white streaming *Light* of the crystal heart of the People. Their eyes are of the Sun. They walk across the green meadow in the Valley of Hope and enter the transporter. The elderguides are silent. Rom sets the course of the transporter.

"We go to Jarlar."

They arrive at the border of the White Man by early late day. There in front of them are two small stone structures with a gate

The Return to the Tombs

in between. On each side of the two stone structures runs a high stone wall as far as the eye can see.

"Did they build this wall to keep themselves in or to keep us out?" speaks one of the chosen.

Rom is silent.

The tranporter slows down as it approaches the gate. Three bewildered guards stand in front. They each carry laser weapons. Rom approaches slowly and carefully.

The guards have never seen a transporter of such age. They walk around to the side where Rom is sitting.

"State your Purpose."

"I am Rom the Elk, the Elderguide of the Earth and Sky of the People of the Sun. We have come to make peace with Jarlar."

৩৯ The Day of the Heart

The guard is silent. He looks into the transporter and walks to the rear and around the transporter. The other guards look curiously but carefully.

"Have you any weapons?"

"We have come to make peace," says Rom. Rom sees that the guard in the small stone structure is on his communicator.

"With Jarlar?" says the guard.

"With the People of the Cities," says Rom.

The guard walks back to the small stone structure and talks with the guard with the communicator. He walks back out and gives a signal. The great steel door swings open.

"Go make your Peace."

They make their way down the straight smooth road. In the distance on the horizon is the hazy outline of the great skyscrapers. The sky is orange. The air begins to taste of chemicals. As they approach the outskirts, they see a large force of soldiers and shocktroopers dressed in battle armor. Three Levitons block the road. Rom slows the transporter and comes to a stop. The Levitons surround the transporter. A large voice blares out of the side of the Leviton.

"Come out of the vehicle with your hands up."

Rom looks back at the six elderguides, "Our time is come."

As they get out of the transporter, the soldiers rush in, knock them to the ground, and bind their arms behind their back. The captain of the soldiers walks over to Rom as he lies face down on the hard surface of the road. He looks down.

"So you have come to make Peace? Search them!" The soldiers roughly run their hands up and down their bodies. They ransack through their pockets. They toss out their bags of necessaries and look through every small thing in them. They rip the soft seats of the transporter. They look in every corner and cavity of the transporter.

"We can find nothing captain ... no weapons, no communicators, and no jewelry."

The captain makes a sign with his head. Rom and the six elderguides are lifted to their feet and placed in the black Leviton.

The Leviton begins to hum as it lifts off from the road and turns

The Return to the Tombs

toward the cities. Rom and the chosen elderguides are silent.

In a little while, Rom feels the bump of the floating Leviton's landing legs touching the earth. The door falls outward from the gray curved wall with a whine. Rom and the elderguides are manhandled to their feet. They walk down and out of the craft. Before them is a great door made of steel. The People of the Sun have been returned to the tombs.

ඟ The Day of the Heart

THE WHIRLWIND

"Jarlar, the Sun People do not have the amulet with them."

Jarlar stares at the display in the war room of Leviton One, his private War Ship. "And, have they been sent to the Tombs?"

"Yes Mr. President." replies Echar.

Jarlar rises from the war table. "We have these Wind People completely in our hands. With no food and water they will come to my terms in a matter of days."

"That is why the delegation from the Sun People came to you."

"They are such a simple naive race. What on earth would make them think I would accept peace? I broke the peace." Jarlar is irritated. "Tell my generals that I will return to the Cities tomorrow. I want to speak to these Sun People."

As the daynight grows old, Rom and the chosen elderguides sit in their cell in the Tombs. The walls are crumbly gray. There is a small dim light in the ceiling of the cell, covered with dirt and cobwebs. They sit in silence. Rom looks through the rusted brown bars into the great darkness. In the dim light, he sees hundreds and hundreds of doors. In every direction, above, below, to one side, and to the other, he sees the dim lights of the cells of the people of the Tombs. It is great dark underground world. He hears the faint cries and moans of those who have found this place to be their place of living. He remembers the stories of how the People of the Sun were freed from the Tombs many, many generations ago. He remembers how they were led away from the Tombs and into the green valleys by the *Ray*. Rom feels the tug of the moon as it finds itself one with the sun.

Rom turns slowly away from the rusted brown bars of the door to the cell. "We approach the time of our giving. Each of you find your place of Wisdom." They sit in silence in their place of wisdom and each find their breath of silence. There is no day in the Tombs, only darkness pierced by the dim light of hope shining faintly from each cell. Even so, Rom feels the turning and knows that the sun and the moon will reveal itself in the new dawn.

ꙮ **The Day of the Heart**

Rom arises and moves to the center of the circle of sitting elderguides. He begins to sing in his deep new found voice. "Oooooooooooom" The sound wafts gently out of the cell and into the silence of the sleeping Tombs. It is consumed in the vastness. Rom takes a deep breath and sings again, "Oooooooooooom". This time two of the chosen elderguides join with him.

"Oooooooooooom" they sing together. As they take another deep breath they hear the song as it returns from the dark gray walls of the Tombs. Two more of the chosen elderguides join the other three on the third breath. "Oooooooooooom." This time the deepness and strength of the song begins to make the walls come alive.

The tombs begin to awake.

As they take their next breath the other two elderguides begin to sing and the song grows. One by one, cell by cell, the people of the Tombs join the song. Rom stands with his hands in the air. The song grows into a great roar. The sound moves through the walls and permeates the air with its richness. They eyes of Rom and the chosen elderguides begin to *Light* up with the brightness that was known at the green meadow in the valley of Hope. Their voices grow deeper and stronger, the tombs begin to vibrate like an instrument of sound. From every cell, the sound grows. It is like the thunder and the great shaking of the earth combined.

Then, a twinkling of *Lights* appear. They moves into the head and down to the spine and up through the heart of each one living and singing in the tombs. The voices of women, and childones, and oldmen, and the dying can be heard in the great chorus. Then the twinklings emerge from each cell and begin to flow into the heart of Rom.

He stands like the Elk as the *Light* force enters his chest. The sound grows even more and Rom begins to shine like the moon. As the *Light* force pours in, every part of his earth form gets brighter and brighter. Then the crystal heart of the White Man begins to stream through his flesh. It grows brighter and brighter.

The dark crumbly walls of the tombs become white with *Light* force.

Every cell is illumined. The darkness is no more. As the *Light*

The Whirlwind

force grows, the great thunderous song grows.

Then, Rom the Elk, takes his hands unto his earth form and brings the streaming crystal heart from his luminous chest and sets it on the white *Light* bars of the cell. The steel doors sing with the walls. Rom's earthform is as clear as the light streaming crystal.

Rom raises his arms high and sings to the sky and then ... he is no more. Every cell door opens. The streaming *Light* of the crystal heart of the White Man has been lit.

The singing gives way to the *White Streaming Light*. The chosen elderguides walk out of their cell and see the white glowing walls of the Tombs. Thousands and thousands appear from their cells. Their clothes are white as washed linen.

The sun and the moon are one.

The Day of the Heart

THE LIBERATION

The sun reveals itself at the turning as Jarlar is awakened.
"Jarlar! We have some major disturbance in the Tombs."

"Make way then," grumbles Jarlar.

As the presidential command ship heads for the Cities, the moon moves into the sun casting its shadow over all of the land. The day turns daynight. Father Wind stops. Then, a great whirlwind of *Light* is seen streaming down from the white rimmed sunmoon. It descends to the earth and to the forces of Jarlar.

As it touches the earth, the levitons of Jarlar and his shocktroopers are lifted up and away from the earth. The whirlwind moves around the great Mesa of Argonon lifting all of Jarlar's forces of war. They spin in the twirling *Light* sky like leaves in a winter wind. Up, they go until they can be seen no more. In a few breathes, they are gone.

As the moon moves out of the sun and its great shadow lifts, the light of day returns. Og looks down from the great earthship Argonon. There below in the fields around Argonon lay only a few parts and pieces of the great force of Jarlar.

Jarlar has been destroyed. The Wind People have seen a great wonder. What miracle of fortune has brought this, thinks Og?

Jarlar arrives in the Cities in his presidential warship and lands at the door to the Tombs. The steel curved door opens with a whir. He takes a few steps down only to stop. Streaming from the cracks between the great gate that leads to the tombs is the strong clear white *Light* of the crystal heart. He walks slowly towards the *Light*.

Echar bolts from the craft and shouts, "Mr. President, we have lost contact with our forces." Jarlar does not hear. He is entranced with the streaming *Light*. It is as if the whole mountain is aglow.

"Open the gate," commands Jarlar.

The Tomb guards shake with fear.

"Open the gate," commands Jarlar.

The Tomb guards look at Jarlar and they look at the streaming *Light*. They run like scared children.

The Day of the Heart

Jarlar walks to the opening, announces the security code and pushes the red button. Alone, he stands at the portal of the Tombs. The black steel doors begin to open. The *Light* force pours out like a great flood over a dam. Jarlar stand motionless with his hands clenched to his side. He stares into the *Light* force as it comes over and surrounds him.

His eyes grow wide and his body trembles.

He lets out a scream. The *Light* force fills the air with its power. It is as bright as bright can be. Nothing but *Light* can be seen. Jarlar's screams continue in the bath of the white *Light*. He can only be heard. The *Light* consumes him. The screaming slowly disappears into the luminous air.

At the portal to the tombs stands the elderguides. Their eyes are full of *Light*, their heartminds are full. The First of the chosen at the green meadow in the Valley of Hope carries the *Light* streaming crystal heart. They walk out of the tombs as their ancestors had walked many generations before. With them is Ren. She stares at the place where Jarlar had stood. She looks down at the earth and into the sky. Jarlar is gone.

She turns and looks back to the portal. The people of the Tombs begin to emerge. They are confused and amazed. Many have not seen the light of day for many many years. They walk by, not knowing why they are free, or who has freed them. They only know of the great thunderous roar of the singing and of the streaming white *Light* that chased the darkness out of the Tombs.

Ren goes to the 6 Elderguides.

"Where is Rom?"

They are silent.

"Where is Rom?"

"He is of the oneness," the first answers. "He brought the crystal heart into the tombs with in his own earthform and was made one with its streaming white *Light*."

Ren is without words. The great crystal heart of the White Man has consumed the man she could not love and the man that she would. Sadness overcomes her.

"Ren!"

Ren looks up. It is Lily and the other elderguides. Lily runs to

The Liberation

Ren. They hold each other for many breaths. "I knew I would see you again," says Lily, full of Joy. "And I knew I would see you sweet Lily." Lily's joy spreads deep into Ren's heart.

Ren rises and speaks with a voice of wisdom," We will go to the palace and be with my People. We will bring the crystal heart and we will place it high so all may view and feel of its streaming white *Light*."

The Day of the Heart

SUN MAN MOON

As the earth finds its shadow from the sun moon, word spreads quickly throughout the Cities of the Liberation of the People of the Tombs, and of the destruction of Jarlar and his forces of war. Ren and the 12 chosen elderguides with Lily and Mark place the light streaming crystal heart on a pole over the balcony that faces the great avenue. Its white *Light* turns the daynight into day. Tens and tens of thousands of the People of the Cities gather to see and feel of its *Light*force. All through the bright daynight, tens of thousands more come to see and bath in its power.

Ren, Lily, Mark, and the 12 chosen elderguides gather in the presidential Office of State. Outside, the People are calling "Isabelle, Isabelle."

"Who do they call for?" asks Lily.

"They call for me," says Ren. "I am the First Lady of the Cities."

"And your name is Isabelle?

"Yes, when you first found me, I told you I was Rain, like Rain from the Sky."

"And so you did not tell the truth."

"I told the truth about Jarlar."

Lily looks into Ren's eyes. "I do not understand."

Ren caresses Lily's wrinkled brow. "Truth is not a simple thing."

Ren walks to the open window that overlooks the great gathering of the People of the Cities and raises both arms upward to the sky. The gathering explodes with delight. The faces of the People are bright with joy.

"I have never known my People to be of such cheer," says Ren to the chosen elderguides. Ren remains at the window waving to the cheering crowd. "Where do we go from here?"

"Our way will be made clear" answers the First of the Twelve. "We will wait for the oneness."

They wait throughout the bright daynight. Lily and Mark find their nightsleep on the soft chairs. The twelve chosen elderguides sit in their circle and seek their place of wisdom as they had in

ꙮ **The Day of the Heart**

the councilmound. Ren stands at the window looking towards the turning.

As the sun reveals itself at the turning, its soft glow lights the face of Ren. The great gathering of the people has grown to many tens of thousands. They are quiet. Their hearts are full of the streaming white *Light* of the crystal heart.

Then, the unseen new moon arrives at the turning. Ren is transfixed. She sees a small speck of shining light in the unseen newness. It seems like a distant faint star. As the turning brings the moon and the sun higher into the sky, the faint star grows brighter. Ren watches. Her heart quickens. The star grows in its intensity. Closer and closer it comes.

"It is a great starship!"

Ren watches as it enters the clear blue sky creating waves of vibrating light and sound. Down to earth it comes. As it slowly descends on the grounds before the palace, the people scatter, yet they are not afraid. Its great shadow is lost in the streaming white *Light* of the crystal heart. It hovers like a Leviton just above the ground. The twelve elderguides arise from their circle. " It is the Oneness" says the first. Lily and Mark awake from their chairs.

Ren's heart is overflowing. They all stand at the great open window. The luminous form of the starship opens and a great stairway extends down to the open window. Ren feels the turning. There in the doorway stands a man with eyes like the sun.

It is Rom.

Ren runs up the ramp of the Starship as Rom smiles and rushes down to greet her.

Rom and Ren embrace with a kiss that lasts many breaths.

"What are they doing?" says Lily.

"They are kissing," says Mark.

"Why?"

Mark looks at Lily with that special smile. "I think that's called Love."

Sun Moon Man

THE END OF THE TELLING

Rom and Ren were married in the green meadow in the Valley of Hope. Their union brought the union of all the Peoples. The White Man of the Cities quit burning rocks and rock oil. The Wind People rebuilt their energy lands in the wilderness and made energy enough for the Cities. The People of the Moon returned to space with the White Man's poisons and sent them into the sun where they were destroyed forever. The People of the Sun continued to live "the way" that was given to them when they were first freed from the Tombs. They remained in balance with the earth and all of its creatures. They did begin to journey from their Valleys and they began to allow visitors into their Valleys. They even allowed their children to watch the movies of the other Peoples.

And, they learned to love, not just the oneness, but each other.

To this day, the streaming white *Light* Crystal Heart of the People of the Sun remains in the green meadow in the Valley of Hope.

The Crystal Heart of the White Man shines brightly over the Palace of the People of Earth. The treaty that was broken was forgotten. People of Peace need no Treaty.

"And what of Lily and Mark, Grandmother?"

They were married in the Palace once they grew to the age of loving. They had three children. The youngest of those had two children. The oldest of those two is … me.

"You mean this story is true?"

"Truth is not a simple thing."

The Day of the Heart

About The Author

Michael J. Osborne is a author, inventor, clean energy policy maker, and climate change activist. Presently, he works in Austin, Texas where he is helping the local electric utility become the leading green utility in the country. He has served under two Texas governors on the State of Texas Energy Planning Partnership, the Texas Sustainable Energy Development Council, and the Texas Energy Coordination Council. Locally, he has served as Chairman of the City of Austin Resource Management Commission.

He is a founder of the Texas Renewable Energy Industries Association and has worked for three decades in the Renewable Energy industry. His other works include *Lightland, Climate Change and the Human Potential*, and *Silver in the Mine*, both available on Amazon and at Bookstores.

He is a recognized visionary in the fields of energy and human settlement.

About the Artist

Charlie Loving was born in London in 1941 during the Blitz. He started drawing at age 2. He has lived in England, France, Switzerland, Ghana, Zaire, Algeria, Columbia, Peru, Vietnam, Real de Catorce, SLP, and Round Rock, Texas. His drawings have appeared in The Rag, the LA Free Press, and the Berkeley Barb. He has a career as a sports writer, a TV weatherman, a radio sports commentator, a mud salesman, and the promoter of the sport of chicken flying. He has a home in Real County with his wife Ray.

www.ingramcontent.com/pod-product-compliance
Lightning Source LLC
Chambersburg PA
CBHW070949080526
44587CB00015B/2245